Managing Reference Today

Managing Reference Today

New Models and Best Practices

Kay Ann Cassell

ROWMAN & LITTLEFIELD
Lanham • Boulder • New York • London

Published by Rowman & Littlefield
A wholly owned subsidiary of The Rowman & Littlefield Publishing Group, Inc.
4501 Forbes Boulevard, Suite 200, Lanham, Maryland 20706
www.rowman.com

Unit A, Whitacre Mews, 26-34 Stannary Street, London SE11 4AB

British Library Cataloguing in Publication Information Available

Library of Congress Cataloging-in-Publication Data Available

ISBN 9781538101674 (hardback : alk. paper) | ISBN 9780810892217 (pbk. : alk. paper) | ISBN 9780810892224 (electronic)

♾ ™ The paper used in this publication meets the minimum requirements of American National Standard for Information Sciences Permanence of Paper for Printed Library Materials, ANSI/NISO Z39.48-1992.

Printed in the United States of America

Contents

Preface

I continually hear librarians say that they don't do reference anymore, and I think, *How can that be possible?* Well, maybe they don't have a print reference collection and maybe they don't have a reference desk, but I bet they still answer reference questions and help their users. So I first began by developing a PowerPoint presentation about all the ways librarians are answering reference questions beyond the reference desk. As I began to look at the research on reference service, I began to see the richness of this research and how much it was telling us about reference service—both why traditional reference service is hanging on and why we need to abandon the reference desk and move on to other ways of providing reference service. This book is an attempt to show both where reference service comes from and where it is going. It is not a straight path forward, but there is lots of interesting research that points us in new creative directions for moving forward. We can better serve our users and make our case for why reference service is still needed.

I think *Managing Reference Today: New Models and Best Practices* will be useful to practitioners who see their demand for reference lessening and want to try something new. The research shows there are lots of ways to proceed that have already been tested and found to work. Regardless of the type of library, the librarian will find useful information. It will also be useful to library schools as they teach their students. Those students dreaming of sitting behind a reference desk and answering questions need to understand that times have changed. Reference is more active, and the expectations of users are very different. Sitting at a desk is usually the last resort.

Managing Reference Today: New Models and Best Practices covers many aspects of reference service from the many reference service models— the traditional reference desk to outreach and social media. Reference service now freed from the reference desk by the new online resources can be performed anywhere. Libraries have moved sometimes cautiously into the new models of reference. But the research shows that there are many new models that work well and that the users are easily converted. I hope that the very positive research in this book will encourage librarians to move away from the reference desk and try newer models of reference service. Librarians have a more dynamic role in reference than what we have played. We can do much more and must do much more if we are to find our place in the new and changing world.

I developed the content by looking at the research available. It is very impressive to see the careful research done by librarians in the United States and elsewhere documenting the ways reference service can and should change. Libraries need to move forward using this research and doing their own. Many say that librarians do not need to sit at a reference desk, but what should they be doing? I hope this book answers some of the questions.

Chapter 1 looks back at where reference comes from and how it progressed to the present. Ironically, reference has not changed very much except to add online resources and better technology.

Chapter 2 looks at recent reference models that have been developed, such as tiered reference, roving reference, consultation services, learning commons, and even a no-desk model.

Chapter 3 looks at new reference services that have been developed mostly due to virtual technology. This includes chat reference, texting, e-mail, twitter, and mobile services.

Chapter 4 looks at staffing models. It discusses how libraries have changed using more paraprofessionals to answer basic reference questions and many models in between. The introduction of the personal librarian in academic libraries has been developed in academic libraries. Staffing virtual reference is also discussed.

Chapter 5 looks at outreach. Outreach goes beyond the four walls of the library to reach new audiences. Each type of library has a different way of doing outreach. Outreach has become an important component of library service—both bringing new audiences into the library and going out to talk to the members of the library's community.

Chapter 6 looks at the training of reference librarians. Much has had to change as print collections disappear and electronic collections replace them. The skills needed by librarians have also changed.

Chapter 7 looks at assessment and evaluation. In general, assessment and evaluation play an important role in reference services. We need to know how the users see our services and whether there are ways to improve them. There are both quantitative and qualitative techniques for finding out more about how our reference services are used.

Chapter 8 looks at collections. As our collections become more electronic, we have to look at them differently. They require more careful evaluation and more careful selection due to their cost.

Chapter 9 sums up the book. Where are we going with reference service and why? It is obvious that the users have a different point of view about libraries in the age of the Internet, Google, Wikipedia, and so forth. So is there still something libraries can provide that is different? My answer is a definite yes. Libraries can provide customized services to users going beyond Google and the Internet. But we must market these services if we want to maintain our user base. We must articulate to our users what library reference service can do for them that is different from the Internet and Google.

I hope that readers of this book will want to examine the way they provide reference service and decide to try at least one new idea. Reference service has a great deal of potential, and librarians have a great deal to share with their patrons. Many libraries are already expanding their services to meet the needs of patrons with a wide variety of information needs. The future of reference service is based on identifying information needs and going beyond the basics to fulfill them.

Acknowledgments

I would like to acknowledge the excellent work of my research assistant, Vanessa Kitzie, who has worked tirelessly with me to bring this book to completion. Also thanks to the faculty and students in the Department of Library and Information Science at Rutgers University who are a constant source of information and inspiration.

Chapter One

Understanding Reference Services and Collections Today

As librarians we have paid attention to developing our collections and correctly answering questions from our patrons. Discussion has taken place regarding how we provide reference services (it is scattered throughout the literature); however, the development of new service models has not taken a strong hold in the profession. Some librarians continue to hold on to the traditional reference desk model whereas others have moved on to completely eliminate the reference desk. Many variations of these models also exist. For these reasons, more examination is needed of what our patrons really need and want, and how we can best serve them in this changing information environment. This book aims to move our thinking forward and point us in new directions. Reference services need not be abandoned, but they do need to be redesigned and refocused to meet our patrons' needs.

Our work has become more challenging as collections rapidly change, the amount of information sources expand, and new ways of communicating are available, thanks to emerging technology. These changes have caused librarians to rethink the way we provide services. Our patrons can answer many questions for themselves through the Internet. So what is left for librarians are often the more difficult questions. What does this changing landscape mean in terms of how librarians should provide reference services? In order to understand this question, it is important to look back at where we have been as well as forward to both engage with the future and develop new ways to meet patron needs in this changing information climate. At the same time, all libraries do not have the same group of patrons, so some libraries are changing faster than others. For this reason, there is no one right way forward. Nevertheless, it is important to continually evaluate how we are providing services to our patrons, how our patrons search for information, and whether our reference services reflect the needs of our patron groups.

In this chapter we will look at the history of reference services and their early development. Then we will explore changes in reference services beginning in the 1970s. Decade by decade we will look at how reference services have expanded. With changes in reference services have come changes in their location, staffing, and range of services and activities provided. This overview set the stage for a discussion in other chapters of present-day services and activities, as well as what the future holds.

HISTORY OF REFERENCE SERVICE

Reference services were introduced by Samuel Green, who decided to provide them at the Worchester (Massachusetts) Public Library in 1876. Green rationalized these services by noting that "persons who use a popular library for purposes of investigation generally need a great deal of assistance."[1] Such assistance, as conceived of by Green, was geared toward those who might not have the privilege or position to accomplish information-based goals: "When scholars and persons of high social position come to a library, they have confidence enough, in regard to the cordiality of their reception, to make known their wishes without timidity or reserve. Modest men in the humbler walks of life, and well-trained boys and girls, need encouragement before they become ready to say freely what they want."[2] To this end, Green saw the librarian as one who welcomed patrons and made them feel comfortable in the library. He encouraged librarians to develop good relations with their patrons in an effort to meet the patrons' need for information, stating that "a librarian should be as unwilling to allow an inquirer to leave the library with his question unanswered as a shop-keeper is to have a customer go out of his store without making a purchase."[3] Green also taught librarians how to instruct patrons to use the library, answer their questions, and help them find good information sources. He envisioned reference services as a way to show the community the library's value and hoped that the municipality would provide more money to buy books and fund additional staff positions.[4] Early reference services often included a reader's advisory service, although this service became an offshoot of reference services as time passed. In fact, some libraries such as the New York Public Library later set up a separate office where patrons could come, talk with a librarian, and leave with a list of recommended books to read.[5]

The idea of reference services caught on quickly. At the university level, Melvil Dewey established a reference department at Columbia College (now Columbia University) in 1884. Other libraries followed suit. In 1915 at the American Library Association (ALA) meeting, W. W. Bishop, the superintendent of the Reading Room of the Library of Congress, delivered a seminal paper on "The Theory of Reference Work." In this paper, Bishop defined reference work as "the service rendered by a librarian in the aid of some sort of study" and as "an organized effort on the part of libraries in aid of the most expeditious and fruitful use of their books."[6] Like Green, Bishop envisioned the role of the librarian "to make books useful and more used."[7] Library schools began to teach reference soon after World War I.

In 1923, Charles Williamson issued a report, *Training for Library Service: A Report Prepared for the Carnegie Corporation of New York*, which made the argument that formal training was needed for a librarian. At this time "only two library schools required the completion of a bachelor's degree for admission, the University of Illinois Library School and the New York State Library School."[8] Williamson also outlined core competencies required by librarians and "published in his report a course description for reference work in an attempt to define the scope and content of the curricula of library schools."[9] In this description, Williamson said that "the aim of this course is not only to give the student some idea of the method of handling books [but also] to familiarize him with the use of indexes, table of contents, and varying forms of arrangement, and finally to suggest some method of comparison and evaluation."[10] This description reflects an emphasis on reader advisory as a key element of reference service.

James I. Wyer wrote the first major reference textbook, *Reference Work: A Textbook for Students of Library Work and Librarians*, published by the ALA in 1930, in which he developed a theory of reference service. Similar to Williamson, Wyer also supported the idea of formal training to become a librarian and specified that a graduate degree in a subject area and library training should be required to excel at reference work. He also went beyond the popular conception of reference as reader's advisory by proposing three levels of library service: conservative, moderate, and liberal. At the conservative level, the librarian does not find answers to questions but organizes reference materials effectively and teaches patrons to help themselves.[11] The moderate level of reference services provides fact-finding or searching for answers to questions, where the librarians are "at hand to produce books, to help, to explain, and suggest, and sometimes merely to listen."[12] The final, liberal level suggests that the librarian answer each question the patron poses by doing whatever might be necessary. Wyer urged that librarians aspire to the liberal level of reference work. Samuel Rothstein later built upon Wyer's idea but called the three levels minimal, middling, and maximum. At the minimal level, librarians should instruct patrons to become self-sufficient, while at the maximum level, librarians were to emphasize the delivery of information to the patron. Despite these calls for an expansion in the breath of reference services offered, libraries continued to offer minimal service to be egalitarian in regard to the service that was provided.[13]

Another reference textbook, written by Margaret Hutchins and titled *Introduction to Reference Work*, was published by the ALA in 1944. Hutchins, an assistant professor at the School of Library Service at Columbia University, took an even broader view of reference work, including an in-depth discussion about "principles and methods of reference work in general,"[14] coining the phrase "reference interview,"[15] and stressing the importance of approachability among librarians.[16]

As the breadth of reference services continued to be advanced theoretically but less so in practice, reference collections changed. Due to technological advances, librarians were able to move from predominately print collections to collections with some print materials and a growing number of online reference resources by 2000. These advances began in the 1970s, when indexes started to be offered online through Dialog, BRS (Bibliographic Retrieval Service), and SDC (Systems Development Corporation). Initially, the library paid by the search, and then with the introduction of these systems on CD-ROMs in the 1980s, the library could pay a flat fee. CD-ROM technology made a tremendous difference in patron satisfaction as patrons could now work on their own. The Internet furthered this autonomy by making it possible for databases to be more widely available to patrons by the library paying an annual subscription fee. This development has meant that databases and online reference resources have become more patron-friendly—the patrons can now do their own searching with little assistance from the librarian or library staff member, and the databases can be used by multiple patrons at the same time. As would be expected, an increase in patron autonomy has led to a current climate in which reference books and services are perceived by some library patrons to be unnecessary or require too much time to use. More discussion on collections will take place in chapter 8.

In their article "The Shape of Services to Come: Values-Based Reference Services for the Largely Digital Library," Chris Ferguson and Charles Bunge nicely sum up some of the transformations in reference services outlined so far. Specifically, the authors identify "the major dimensions along which change has occurred" in reference service models as "the location for providing assistance, staffing configurations, and the services and activities involved."[17] These elements provide a good way to look at how reference services have changed over time, given that the authors frame them as "enduring basics" of how libraries should provide services, regardless of the medium through which these services are provided.[18]

LOCATION OF REFERENCE SERVICE

Amazingly little changed in reference services in the first hundred years after Samuel Green introduced the concept—librarians continued to staff the reference desk and wait for patrons to approach them with questions. The changes that did occur were that reference desks became more elaborate and were often double-staffed to accommodate business volume. Further, librarians articulated the need for librarians, rather than paraprofessionals or students, to staff the reference desk since even a simple reference question might turn into another, more complex one. The maintenance of a traditional reference model signified the continued dependency of patrons on librarians to help them navigate the many print reference sources. Even with new technology, librarians adopted a fairly traditional approach to reference services, though patrons began to find answers to some of their questions on the Internet.

The Reference Desk

Perhaps the most traditional signifier of reference services is the reference desk, which has been the main point of reference services since its inception. Even as the ways in which information is presented, found, and used have changed, librarians have felt that sitting at the reference desk in a visible place was enough to both promote the service and best serve patrons. In 1986, Barbara Ford questioned the view that the reference desk should be the center of reference services in academic libraries, given the changing technologies and strategies both patrons and librarians were using to find and access information.[19] Over a decade later, Marcella Genz in 1998 argued that

> the sorts of problems that can be considered based on the model of the reference desk are simple at best. . . . Much of reference culture revolves around ready reference—something that is easily looked up or referred to rather than those complex information problems that require filtering, analysis, and synthesis. . . . There is a sense of simplicity here which does not recognize that information needs can be complex.[20]

In proposing what librarians should do, if not sit at the reference desk, Karen Summerhill in 1994 suggested that libraries could separate the reference service from the desk. She thought that developing a consultation service as do professionals in other fields, such as lawyers and professors, would give needed status to librarians.[21] Keith Ewing and Robert Hauptman, David Lewis, Steven Bell, and many others have called for the elimination of the reference desk.[22] Yet even with the Internet, which gave many patrons the ability to answer ready reference questions on their own, many librarians preferred to continue to maintain the reference desk as the predominant means to answer questions. This preference stemmed from librarians feeling it was important to be on the front lines giving personal, face-to-face service to patrons. In the current reference environment, only slight modifications appear to be made to reference desk services with most librarians not giving up the reference desk. For example, some have combined it with the circulation desk or with other services. [23]

Changing Mediums to Deliver Reference Services

Although the physical location of the reference desk has continued to be a mainstay in most libraries, other communication mediums have also been employed to deliver reference services. First, a telephone reference service was added as patrons called the library instead of actually visiting the library. Some large public libraries even developed a telephone reference department to answer the many questions coming from this medium. By the 1950s, telephone reference was an additional part of the library's reference services. Mostly short-answer questions, such as ready reference ones, were answered by telephone. These reference requests might be followed up by the patron visiting the library or the library mailing information to the patron. Some public libraries became known for their telephone reference services, such as the Enoch Pratt Public Library in Baltimore and the New York Public Library. In addition to telephone, mail became an asynchronous means through which to send a reference request. Patrons of mail-based reference services were usually people who lived at a distance but had a question that required information about the area in which the physical library was situated, such as information about a local business.

By 1990 librarians began to experiment with other ways of serving patrons, in regard to both the breadth of service types provided and the media by which these services were offered. In regard to service types, Virginia Massey-Burzio introduced the tiered reference model both at Brandeis University and later at Johns Hopkins University. Within this model, Massey-Burzio recognized that patrons needed different levels of service depending on their question. She replaced the traditional reference desk with an information desk staffed by Brandeis graduate students and a research consultation service office staffed by librarians. The information desk answered directional and brief information requests that took less than three minutes. If the patron needed more extensive assistance, they would be referred to a librarian in the research consultation service office. When the librarian was not available, Massey-Burzio specified that "the Information Desk student fills out a 'Request for Information' sheet to be given to the librarian later. Clients are given the option of waiting, returning later or leaving a telephone number where they can be reached." [24] This model countered historical arguments made by librarians of staffing the reference desk with professionals only, and instead emulated the academic model of students visiting a professor's office for assistance. Based on speaking with library staff and students, Massey-Burzio argued that this new model provided better-quality reference services given the traditional reference desk is not designed for in-depth assistance; made better use of staff since simple questions could be answered by the graduate students rather than librarians; improved the image of the professional librarian because the reference encounter would now be more professional in tone and demeanor; and provided more job satisfaction since librarians were more challenged to use their expertise. She stated that "this reference model seems to significantly improve the quality of the interaction between the client and the reference librarian. The privacy and quiet of the research consultation office and the focused attention of a recognized professional seem to be the key to its success."[25] Many libraries have since adopted some form of tiered-reference services that might be a reference desk staffed by paraprofessionals and a consultation service.

Technology also expanded the possibilities for answering reference questions, first with e-mail in the 1990s. E-mail was fast and free, and patrons could, using e-mail, obtain more information than by telephone and information more quickly than via physical mail. Soon library services began to develop e-mail reference services such as the Internet Public Library (IPL), which was developed at the University of Michigan library school, accepted questions from anyone, and had developed a directory of quality websites that could be consulted by the public. As good as e-mail was and is, it is not synchronous, so there is no way for the librarian to clarify the patron's question and to "talk" with the patron in real time. E-mail continues to be offered by libraries for their patrons who wish to communicate by this medium.

Patrons' desire for communication in real time, without needing to physically visit the library or use the telephone, led to libraries' development of live chat services. These services were already being used by companies to communicate with their patrons online. To provide chat services, libraries use free technology, such as LibraryH3lp, and commercial technology, such as QuestionPoint. Some libraries independently provide these services while others join a consortium, especially ones set up by states such as Colorado and Maryland. The advantages of consortia are that by working together, librarians can provide continuous service via chat across time zones.

Other Changes in Reference Services Provision

Once research began to show that not every patron was comfortable approaching the reference desk, librarians began to experiment with other means by which to assist patrons. One approach was roving, where librarians roam the stacks and computer workstations to see if any patrons require help. Roving services did not appear to take away from information exchanged at the reference desk, with a 1996 article by Eileen Kramer noting that the questions she received while roving were more in depth than those asked at the reference desk.[26] Roving was and continues to be advantageous with the introduction of computers into libraries since patrons in need of assistance may be unwilling to leave a library computer to find a librarian, given that they will give up their access to this computer. As librarians began to experiment with roving among the computers and asked if patrons using them needed assistance, some librarians documented what they learned from these experiences to inform other practitioners considering adopting the roving model.[27]

Another popular change for reference services is the move toward a single point of service where libraries combine reference, circulation, and other services into one desk. The choice to adopt this single point of service means that patrons experience less confusion of where they should go within the library based on their information need and also alleviates the number of staff members required to provide the service. Further discussion on how the reference desk is changing can be found in chapter 2.

STAFFING

Staffing has been a point of discussion among librarians over the decades, and the shifting nature of this discussion has directly impacted decisions made about reference services. Early in the development of libraries there was no distinction in library titles. However, beginning with Williamson's report in 1923, there was a clear call made by librarians for having two categories of personnel: clerical workers and librarians. This distinction derived from Williamson's argument that librarians should have a bachelor's degree, followed by formal training at a library school. Through the years, the emphasis on professional librarians continued as graduate schools of librarianship developed throughout the United States. However, the tightening of funding in the 1980s meant that some libraries could not afford as many librarians as in the past. As a result, many libraries began to rethink their staffing, recruiting student workers and paraprofessionals. Librarians continued to staff the reference desk even when research indicated that many basic reference questions could be answered by paraprofessionals. Such research includes a study by Martin Courtois and Lori Goetsch, where they interviewed academic librarians in Illinois and documented that many used nonprofessionals to staff the reference desk. Based on these interviews, the authors recommended a "team" approach to reference where a professional and nonprofessional worked together to staff the reference desk, ensuring that more complex reference questions would receive the proper answers from a trained professional. They also recommended more training for nonprofessionals.[28] In her study of information desks staffed by graduate students and nonprofessionals, Beth Woodard also reported that reference responses were more successful when both a librarian and a staff member

Table 1.1.   A timeline of key events in the development of reference services and collections

Date	Event
1876	Samuel Green introduced the first reference desk at the Worchester, MA, public library in 1876.
1884	Melvil Dewey established a reference department at Columbia College.
1915	At the ALA annual meeting, W. W. Bishop delivers a seminal paper entitled "The Theory of Reference Work."
1923	In the report *Training for Library Service: A Report Prepared for the Carnegie Corporation of New York*, Charles Williamson argued that librarians need formal training. He also emphasized the importance of reference services and in particular reader's advisory.
After WWI	Library schools began to teach reference services.
1930	James I. Wyer wrote the first major reference textbook, *Reference Work: A Textbook for Students of Library Work and Librarians*.
1944	Margaret Hutchins coined the phrase "reference interview" and stressed the importance of approachability among librarians.
1950s	Libraries adopted telephone and mail reference services.
1960s	Libraries implemented instruction, or information literacy.
1970s	Indexes are offered online through Dialog, BRS (Bibliographic Retrieval Service) and SDC (Systems Development Corporation). Libraries pay by the search.
1980s	Databases are offered on CD-ROMs. Librarians pay a flat fee. Patrons were able to search on their own. Library funding is tightened, and as a result, libraries increasingly hired student workers and paraprofessionals.
1986	Barbara Ford questioned the view that the reference desk should be the center of reference service in academic libraries.
1990s	Virginia Massey-Burzio introduced the tiered reference model at Brandeis University. Libraries developed e-mail and chat reference services. Libraries developed roaming reference models. Libraries employed the reference desk as a single point of service.
2000	Social media is used for reference.

shared the reference desk.[29] Based on the results of these findings and observations made in practice, in 1963 Barbara Ford (and others since then) argued that basic reference questions did not need the assistance of a reference librarian and, for this reason, could be addressed by paraprofessionals with access to current technology. To this end, she suggested using computers to answer basic questions or providing printed information sheets, with librarians available to consult on more complex questions. [30]

Although these studies have instituted some changes in staffing, many librarians still clung to their reference desk duties. Recently, Julie Banks and Carl Pracht surveyed 101 academic libraries regarding their staffing of the reference desk and use of nonprofessionals. They found that "[62] percent of the respondents use (non-degreed personnel) at the reference desk and 38 percent do not." Their results also indicated that "62 percent of those who employ nonprofessionals have been using them only for the last ten years or less." [31] Among the libraries that used nonprofessionals at the reference desk, the authors found that they received at least some training. Findings also revealed that "it is definitely standard practice to use nonprofessionals at the reference desk even when no backup (i.e., a librarian) is available." [32] An exemplar model that utilizes paraprofessionals at the reference desk is employed by the University of Arizona Libraries, with librarians available on call or for referral. [33] Further information on these new staffing models will be discussed in chapter 4.

REFERENCE SERVICES AND ACTIVITIES

In addition to providing general reference assistance, libraries have expanded their services over the decades. What began as a single service soon became specialized as both academic and public libraries developed subject reference departments. These provided patrons with more in-depth services. Other services developed include library instruction, virtual reference, use of mobile devices, use of social media, outreach, and more.

Library Instruction

Library instruction has been discussed by the profession for many years. The first librarians to formally implement library instruction were school and academic librarians. Also now known as information literacy, library instruction began in the late 1960s and early 1970s. One of the early leaders in this area was Patricia Knapp at Monteith College (part of Wayne State University) who experimented with developing course-related library assignments based on feedback derived from her working with the faculty. She found that students needed to understand the organization of academic disciplines as well as understand how the library functioned. She also found that students needed to relate the skills they were learning to the importance of why they are learning them. [34]

Information literacy has continued to develop through the decades and now plays a major role in the services provided by academic librarians—both as an educational tool and as a way to provide reference assistance. Although information literacy is often considered a group service, that is, the librarian visits a classroom for a presentation on the library, a great deal of information-literacy instruction is actually done at the reference desk. In the course of helping patrons to find the information they need, librarians may explain how they found the information and the sources used so the patrons will begin to understand how to start their search the next time. Therefore, information-literacy instruction keys into one of the tenants espoused by Green when first introducing the concept of reference services by teaching patrons skills that would allow them to fulfill information-based goals with greater ease and autonomy.[35]

Online chat reference also offers the opportunity to provide library instruction. Many articles have documented the effective use of instruction in chat reference. For example, Patricia Johnston found that within the University of New Brunswick's digital reference services, "60 percent of queries contain some instruction element."[36] The author stated that "synchronous online chat software also makes it easy to instruct patrons on database searching, electronic journals, search strategies and other online information services as if they actually stood at the reference desk."[37]

Embedded Reference

The adoption of online chat reference services is due, at least in part, to the need for assisting patrons in less traditional ways. Delivering community-oriented services is referred to as embedded librarianship, defined by David Shumaker as follows: "Embedded librarians prefer to anticipate information and knowledge needs, work with a team of collaborators, work within a customized service model, emphasize the project over the transaction, and share with their team partners the responsibility for the overall outcome of a project."[38] Jeremie Clyde and Jennifer Lee further define embedded librarianship as "a form of library service customized to a particular community, as opposed to standardized instruction and reference services that may not also be relevant to patron needs."[39] The authors described several embedded librarianship case studies at the University of Calgary, where librarians have fostered research relationships with faculty and students. In each case, they have documented that for librarians, "going out into student and faculty spaces has strengthened the relationship between the librarian and the library patrons."[40] Initially the librarians offered office hours in the department's space and customized library services. Over time, the librarians have furthered the scope of their service, becoming liaisons to the department community by increasing their contact with faculty and students, serving often on departmental committees and attending social events. Each liaison customizes their relationship to their department, which may mean offering reference and collection services, research services, or other services particular to the specific department. Many factors influence how embedded librarianship works, in particular the personalities of the librarian and those they serve. Further information about embedded librarianship, as well as on information literacy as a reference service, will be provided in chapter 5.

Creating Additional Spaces

In addition to extending the scope and breadth of interactions with patrons, libraries have also created additional spaces where these interactions can take place. For instance, some libraries have created library computer centers, often called information commons, which provide students with the ability to research and write collaboratively by using technologies such as a shared workstation, where students practicing a group presentation can share a screen. Libraries often have a reference desk in the information commons to assist patrons with research and other information needs. The acts of creating new spaces to facilitate patrons' needs and providing reference services to accommodate them represent another departure from the traditional reference desk.

Creating Web Resources

Librarians took advantage of technology to provide services consistently available, such as conveying information on websites. Website content includes tutorials, which provide some basic information, such as an academic library tutorial instructing students on how to research and write papers. In conjunction with tutorials, academic libraries offer guides that provide information on how to search literature within a specific subject area and also curate resources pertaining to this specific area. These guides are referred to as LibGuides and have been developed and standardized by companies, such as Springshare, which offer a standard way to present them. LibGuides provide patrons with a way to begin their investigation of a subject area and can direct further, more in-depth questions to the reference desk or alternate service media (e.g., chat, e-mail).

Outreach

Outreach has taken many forms through the decades. Libraries have been well aware of the need to reach out to patrons who were not coming to the library. Early public library outreach efforts included bookmobiles and reaching out to groups underserved by the library, such as migrant workers, factory workers, and local businesses. Libraries have continued these types of outreach efforts but have also concentrated on familiarizing community members with reference services. The types of community reference services developing in public libraries provide good examples of how effective reference outreach can be.

Many new patrons are now being introduced to reference services. Academic libraries tried various ways to reach students, for example, by having hours in the student center, dorms, or other places where students gather. Librarians also visited academic departments to meet with faculty and graduate students (discussed in the previous "Embedded Reference" section). Findings from best practices indicate that reference work need not be one to one and can instead mean that the librarian works with a group of patrons at once. Further information about outreach services is discussed in chapter 5.

Consultation services that borrow from customer-service principles have sprung up, following Massey-Burzio's lead.[41] Case studies examining the implementation of these services have found that both librarians and patrons experience high levels of satisfaction working in this way and feel that real communication can take place, as well as more in-depth discussion. This service uses the skills of the reference librarian since they have more time allotted to discuss a patron's information needs and could perhaps be incorporated within a tiered reference model. Consultation services and their effectiveness are further discussed in chapter 2.

CONCLUSION

The following chapters discuss in more depth the various aspects of reference services overviewed in this chapter. Specifically, these chapters look at new ways of providing reference service, staffing issues, the changing formats of reference sources, training of staff, and assessment and evaluation. As previously discussed at the beginning of this chapter, it appears that many libraries still have not moved beyond the physical reference desk as a service. At the same time, many interesting pilots are taking place in libraries that are bringing new approaches to reference services. These pilots reflect the reality that our patrons have new information needs in the twenty-first century that require new ways of providing reference services. Reference services need to be updated to reflect this changing environment as we deal with new and changing formats, increasingly desired by patrons who do not have the time or training to sort through the abundance of information sources available.

NOTES

1. Samuel S. Green, "Personal Relations between Librarians and Readers," *American Library Journal* 1, no. 2 (October 1876): 74.

2. Ibid.

3. Ibid., 79.

4. Ibid., 81.

5. Bill Crowley, "Rediscovering the History of Readers Advisory Service," *Public Libraries* 44, no. 1 (2005): 37–41.

6. W. W. Bishop, "The Theory of Reference Work," *Bulletin of the American Library Association* 9, no. 4 (1915): 134, 138.

7. Ibid., 139.

8. Marcella D. Genz, "Working the Reference Desk," *Library Trends* 46, no. 3 (1998): 513.

9. Ibid.

10. Charles C. Williamson, *Training for Library Service: A Report Prepared for the Carnegie Corporation of New York* (Boston: Merrymount, 1923), 14.

11. James I. Wyer, *Reference Work: A Textbook for Students of Library Work and Librarians* (Chicago: American Library Association, 1930), 6–7.

12. Ibid., 9.

13. Samuel Rothstein, "Reference Service: The New Dimension in Librarianship," *College and Research Libraries* 11, nos. 25–26 (January 1967): 14.

14. Margaret Hutchins, *Introduction to Reference Work* (Chicago: American Library Association, 1944), v.

15. Mary Jo Lynch, "Hutchins, Margaret," in *ALA World Encyclopedia of Library and Information Services* (Chicago: American Library Association, 1980), 241–42.

16. Hutchins, *Introduction to Reference Work.*

17. Chris D. Ferguson and Charles A. Bunge, "The Shape of Services to Come: Values-Based Reference Services for the Largely Digital Library," *College and Research Libraries* 58, no. 3 (May 1997): 254.

18. Ibid., 262.

19. Barbara J. Ford, "Reference Beyond (and Without) the Reference Desk," *College and Research Libraries* 47, no. 5 (1986): 491.

20. Genz, "Working the Reference Desk," 523.

21. Karen S. Summerhill, "The High Cost of Reference: The Need to Reassess Services and Service Delivery," *Reference Librarian* 20, no. 43 (1994): 71–85.

22. Keith Ewing and Robert Hauptman, "Is Traditional Reference Services Obsolete?" *Journal of Academic Librarianship* 21, no. 1 (1995): 3–6; David W. Lewis, "Traditional Reference Is Dead, Now Let's Move on to Important Questions," *Journal of Academic Librarianship* 21, no. 1 (1995): 10–12; Steven J. Bell, "Who Needs a Reference Desk?" *Library Issues: Briefings for Faculty and Administrators* 27, no. 6 (2007): 1–4.

23. See Juliet Rumble, "The Integrated Services Model: Information Commons in Libraries," in *Reference Reborn: Breathing New Life into Public Services Librarianship*, ed. Diane Zabel, 43–60 (Santa Barbara: Libraries Unlimited, 2011); Carla J. Stoffle and Cheryl Cuillier, "Student-Centered Services and Support: A Case Study of the University of Arizona Libraries' Information Commons," *Journal of Library Administration* 50, no. 2 (2010): 117–34.

24. Virginia Massey-Burzio, "Reference Encounter of a Different Kind: A Symposium," *Journal of Academic Librarianship* 18, no. 5 (1992): 278.

25. Ibid., 279.

26. Eileen H. Kramer, "Why Roving Reference: A Case Study in a Small Academic Library," *Reference Services Review* 24, no. 3 (1996): 67–80.

27. Martin P. Courtois and Maira Liriano, "Tips for Roving Reference: How to Best Serve Library Patrons," *College and Research Libraries News* 61, no. 4 (2000): 289–315.

28. Martin P. Courtois and Lori A. Goetsch, "Use of Nonprofessionals at Reference Desks," *College and Research Libraries* 45, no. 5 (May 1984): 385–91.

29. Beth S. Woodard, "The Effectiveness of an Information Desk Staffed by Graduate Students and Nonprofessionals," *College and Research Libraries* 50, no. 4 (1989): 455–67.

30. Ford, "Reference Beyond," 491.

31. Julie Banks and Carl Pracht, "Reference Desk Staffing Trends: A Survey," *Reference and Patron Services Quarterly* 48, no. 1 (2008): 56.

32. Ibid., 57.

33. Stoffle and Cuillier, "Student-Centered Services."

34. Patricia B. Knapp, "The Reading of College Students," *Library Quarterly: Information, Community, Policy* 38, no. 4 (1968): 301–8.

35. Green, "Personal Relations."

36. Patricia E. Johnston, "Digital Reference as an Instructional Tool: Just in Time and Just Enough," *Searcher* 11, no. 3 (2003): 31.

37. Ibid., 32.

38. David Shumaker, "The Embedded Librarians," *Online* 36, no. 4 (2012): 24.

39. Jerremie Clyde and Jennifer Lee, "Embedded Reference to Embedded Librarianship: 6 Years at the University of Calgary," *Journal of Library Administration* 51, no. 4 (2011): 398.

40. Ibid.

41. Massey-Burzio, "Reference Encounter."

Chapter Two

Moving toward New Models of Reference Services

As discussed in chapter 1, the reference desk model that has been with us since the middle of the nineteenth century has served as the traditional way of structuring reference services. Librarians have been taught that sitting at the reference desk and looking ready to help is the best way of providing service. Beginning in the 1980s some librarians began talking about the need to change. Those discussing these changes included Barbara Ford and Steven J. Bell, who both questioned assumptions of the reference desk as central to reference services; Keith Ewing and Robert Hauptman, who examined the influence of technology on these services; and Karen S. Summerhill, who challenged traditional service-delivery models.[1] Change has not been fast. The model of the reference desk has been easy to maintain and administer so it has held on over time, even though many have suggested that it needs to change or at least be reconfigured.

Several reasons exist for this change. First, all patrons do not come to a reference desk for assistance. Time and again studies have shown that many people find the reference desk too intimidating, think it is only for quick questions, or have sensitive information needs that they would prefer to express anonymously and, therefore, will try to find their information on their own. Second, information is now available in many formats, and the way it can be delivered has changed enormously in the past two decades. Technology has made it possible to communicate with patrons by e-mail, chat, instant messaging (IM), text, and more, and thus has the potential to reach new patrons outside of the physical space of the library. This emerging technology combined with the expectations of patrons to be able to get information whenever and wherever they decide they need it is changing the face of reference service. Third, there exists a mismatch between patron and librarian mental models of reference services. Patrons have in their minds an idea of what kinds of information and services are available at the reference desk. This mind-set is often related to other desks or counters they use, such as an information desk in a store or a walk-up window for a government service where the questions and services available are short from both length- and time-based perspectives. In contrast, librarians are trained to conduct lengthy reference interviews, which while appropriate for certain types of questions, runs into contention with patron expectations of timeliness in receiving desired information.

The traditional reference desk service flies in the face of what is known about what service people expect and want and what draws them to the library. Meanwhile, nationally known companies provide an experience for their users that adds more value when compared to how many libraries provide service. Going into almost any store will give us some ideas about what these companies think will make their patrons remember them and come back. Maybe it is a welcoming person as patrons enter the store, maybe it is the extra-special service they receive, maybe it is a thank-you for using the service, or maybe it is something companies do for patrons that is different and completely unexpected. What we can learn from these observations is that individuals respond to the entire customer service experience; in a library, this experience goes beyond just helping patrons answer their questions. The patron will be more apt to continue using a particular service if they have been provided with some value-added elements that make the experience more than a routine transaction. Librarians do talk about value-added services, yet when patrons contact them, they often do not go beyond the basics, for example, conducting a lengthy reference interview. This routine service may make patrons think that there is no reason to contact the library since they could have found similar information on the Internet. In terms of the reference desk, we should be asking ourselves, does the whole layout of the reference desk influence this service and is the desk getting in our way? Maybe librarians need to think about how we work with patrons in ways that are less defined by traditional reference services and more suited to the individual needs of the patrons. Do other ways of providing reference services offer more opportunities for developing the patron experience?

In this chapter newer models of reference services are discussed. These models include tiered reference, roving reference, research consultation services, learning commons, and combining points of service. How does each of these models meet patron needs by going beyond the traditional model of reference services? These models show what we have learned both about reference service and our patrons, as well as demonstrate how we must diversify the way we serve our patrons. By being flexible in our implementation of service models, we acknowledge that all patrons are not the same, nor are the ways they should be served.

THE REFERENCE DESK—MOVING FORWARD

As librarians continue to debate the need for the reference desk, those who want to keep it argue that when patrons come to the library, they anticipate and desire human contact. Some librarians whose research has supported this point of view include Karen Sobel, whose study of first-year undergraduates at the University of North Carolina revealed that

> at least in their first year of college, students respond most strongly to library reference service promotions given in person. While conversations between first-year students and library staff at orientation only left a small mark—4.6 percent of students recalled these interactions, discussions held during instruction sessions held major sway over students' choices. First-year students also indicated a preference for face-to-face reference interactions. [2]

This finding indicates that while virtual communication still constitutes a viable option, the physical components of reference services are still necessary to reach specific patron groups, such as first-year undergraduates.

Librarians also want to keep the reference desk as a symbol of their service. Some say that they would not know how to operate without a reference desk. Further, it may be expected by upper-level management that librarians will be visibly providing services to patrons, and staffing a desk fulfills this expectation. Dennis Miles denoted the importance of the physical reference desk in his survey of 119 academic libraries, which found that 66.4 percent still used a reference desk and 77.2 percent staffed the desk with a librarian some or all of the time. [3] Those who did not provide reference from a traditional desk offered services from a shared desk or were on call in their offices. [4] Others have changed to a smaller desk and provide a chair and monitor so that the patron can view the search. Some libraries that have opted for models other than the reference desk have found no decline in the number of reference questions. If patrons needed assistance, they approached whatever kind of desk there was—whether a combined circulation and reference desk or a general information desk. These studies, and those like them, therefore indicate both the importance of physical cues—derived from the face-to-face interactions the desk engenders—and the continued importance of reference services in general. While the reference desk may be considered inefficient in some situations, these cues and services still need to be considered when developing new models.

In addition to concerns about the inefficiency of the reference desk, we have to consider another point made by Miles—that reference work has changed. Where we once made effective use of the reference desk because we selected physical volumes to show to the patron, now libraries have minimal reference collections, and most of our reference service consists of using online resources. [5] That being said, the need for a physically fixed

Figure 2.1.   How a library chose to update its reference desk—old reference desk. *Gwinnett County Public Library (GA)*

reference desk is greatly diminished since patrons may require research assistance at a particular computer terminal or even remotely. This change in reference work does not alleviate the need for reference service, but it does call for a reconsideration of how that service should be provided. It is time to pause and reexamine how we work with patrons. We need to help them sort out the wide variety of information sources that they encounter on the Internet including a steep increase in the number of online serials available and elsewhere. Such assistance is quite different than finding a physical reference book that will answer a question. Now the possibilities are more numerous, and it takes more experience to be able to sort out the right answer for a particular patron.

An example of a library that has adopted a new reference service model can be found at the University of California Library at Merced, which opened a new building in 2005 with no reference desk. Instead, the library has two service points: the library services desk and a library help desk. Both desks are staffed by library student assistants who are carefully trained and can thus handle basic reference questions, freeing up librarians to provide more specialized and in-depth services. When the student assistants have questions beyond their training, they refer the inquiry to a librarian. Outside of the two physical service points, the librarians make every effort to be available to

Figure 2.2. Self checkout machine at the Gwinnett County Public Library.

patrons who have questions and can be contacted by chat reference, text messaging, phone, instant messaging, and e-mail. This model proves effective for the library given that the small librarian staff is busy providing library instruction and giving speeches, so staffing the reference desk is not an option. Since assisting students, faculty, and staff is the main priority of the library, the librarians provide many ways for their patrons to reach them.

Although changing the structure of the reference desk itself has been useful, other ways to meet patrons' needs must be considered. Some libraries have simply added other services but maintained the reference desk, while others have closed the reference desk and moved to new models. These new models include

- tiered reference services;
- expanded electronic reference services (discussed in chapter 3);
- learning commons model;
- research consultation service;
- roving reference; and
- a single service point model.

Figure 2.3.   Self checkout machine at the Gwinnett County Public Library.

TIERED REFERENCE SERVICES

In a tiered reference service, a reference desk remains but only for short-answer questions. Many libraries staff this desk with well-trained paraprofessionals who can refer to the librarian research consultation service questions that are more in depth and require additional time to answer. Tiered reference service thus proves efficient by providing patrons with a choice of service depending on their information needs and by making the best use of the librarians' skills.

Virginia Massey-Burzio identified four issues influencing the development of the tiered reference model: service quality, the best use of staff, the image of professional librarians, and job satisfaction. First of all, she thought that service at the reference desk did not allow librarians to do their best work since the reference desk environment was best for short-answer ques-

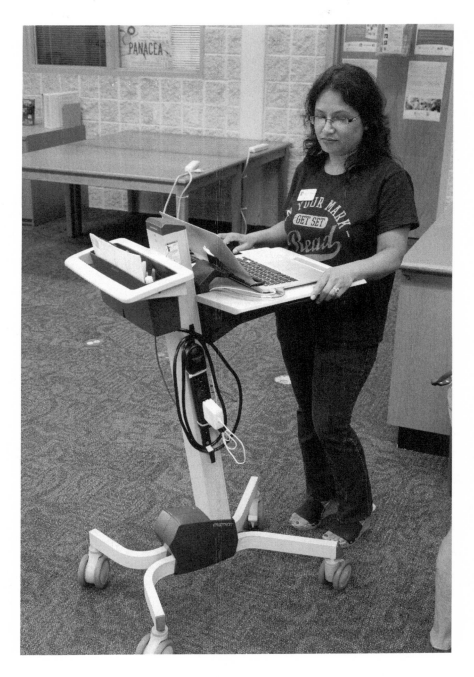

Figure 2.4.   Mobile reference desk at the Gwinnett County Public Library.

Figure 2.5.   A contemporary reference desk.

tions given the high volume of questions asked and patron expectations of questions, even in-depth ones, resolved with a quick reply.[6] This latter finding is supported by Thelma Freides, who suggested that the reference desk can actually act more as an impediment than a facilitator to high-quality assistance because patrons perceive it as intended for simple questions and quick replies. Second, the service at the reference desk did not make the best use of staff since many of the questions at the reference desk could be answered by a well-trained student or nonprofessional. Third, the service at the reference desk did nothing to improve the image of librarians since the reference desk setting does not lend itself to a professional encounter due to presence of visual cues indicating a quick, commercial encounter and lack of visual cues indicating the expertise of the individual staffing the desk. And fourth, service provided at the reference desk did little for librarians' job satisfaction since answering so many simple questions did not challenge them. Simultaneously, patrons did not have the capacity to appreciate the expert services provided by these librarians given the aforementioned limitations.[7]

To address this mismatch between the actual services fulfilled by the reference desk and the level of expertise required to staff it, the California State Polytechnic University Library students trained students to answer basic questions, screen questions, and refer more in-depth questions to reference librarians. The program is called LibStARs (Library Student Assistant Researchers). The training focused on "how to answer directional, printing/copying, facility and services and basic reference questions as well as how to refer questions appropriately to back-up librarians."[8] All transactions are logged to monitor the students' answers. Evaluation of the project has shown the program to be successful with students and patrons. The LibStARs got high marks for approachability and helpfulness with 45.5 percent of students stating their preference for asking for help from a peer. Only 5 percent would have preferred to ask for help from someone other than a peer. This latter finding suggests that redirecting the staffing model of the reference desk toward student workers may increase use of this service by enhancing the perceived approachability of the staff.

The second part of this program was the addition of LibAnswers. Here, librarians populated a database with answers to frequently asked questions. New questions and answers are continually added to the database as a result of e-mails from patrons or based on questions addressed to librarians. Use of LibAnswers has generated an increase in online transactions, suggesting that a previously unmet need for instantaneous delivery of ready reference questions could now be met in a virtual environment.[9]

In another study of the expertise required to staff a reference desk, Pixey Mosley studied questions received by staff at the Texas A&M University Libraries at the desk closest to the door. She found that while a large percentage of questions were directional, many were more in depth, addressing computer issues, subject-specific needs, and research assistance, to name a few. Although the answers to the majority of questions asked at the front desk were correct (74 percent), a disparity was present between the high accuracy of answers to ready reference questions, such as directional ones, versus more in-depth ones. Even when performing referrals to subject specialists, front-desk staffers, who tended to be students or paraprofessionals, tended to refer to the incorrect librarian. Findings from this study indicate that while a tiered reference model may constitute an appropriate means through which to address specific types of reference-based needs and balance limited resources, implementation of this approach requires planning to address consequences derived by its limitations. For this reason, Mosley recommended training staff to conduct a basic reference interview and identify when a patron should be referred to a librarian, modifying patron expectations by reconfiguring the desk or signage, or using more experienced staff at the front desk. The choice of which recommendation to take will depend on types of services provided, patron expectations, and resources available.[10]

Variations of tiered reference service have also been tried. Sometimes libraries have three levels of service: a general information desk where patrons enter the library, a reference desk for routine and ready reference questions, and a research consultation service for more in-depth assistance. Many libraries now offer research consultation services in both academic and public contexts, such as Kent State University Library (Ohio), Barnard College Library (New York), and Arlington Heights Memorial Library (Illinois). These consultation services offer patrons an opportunity to sit down with a librarian and get more individualized assistance. The service is often listed on the library's website so that patrons can make appointments in advance of their visit. It can also give librarians a chance to prepare for the research consultation if patrons give them some information when they make appointments. Appointments are not necessary in many libraries, so patrons can be easily referred from the reference desk to the research consultation service. Miles found that 87 percent of libraries surveyed offered research consultation services.[11] The research consultation service signals another step in the services provided at the library. It is a more personal and professional approach to reference service.

Tiered reference moves away from the single reference desk model. It sends a message to patrons that they can expect more in-depth service at the library and not just answers to ready reference questions. The research consultation service, provided as part of many tiered reference services, gives value-added service to patrons so they will have higher expectations of the extent of assistance they can receive at the library.

Some guidelines for developing a tiered reference service follow:

1. Decide who will staff the reference desk. Will it be all paraprofessionals or a mix of paraprofessionals and librarians?
2. Provide training for paraprofessionals and continuous follow-up training to ensure that referrals are being appropriately made as needed.
3. Do periodic patron evaluations to be sure that the service at the reference desk is meeting patron expectations.
4. Restrict the types of questions paraprofessionals can answer at the reference desk, and carefully outline the types of questions that should be referred.
5. Make sure that librarians are available for the research consultation service at whatever hours are advertised.

INFORMATION/LEARNING COMMONS MODEL

As the number of services provided by libraries has increased, in part due to heightened technology use, information or learning commons have been a way to centralize information and technology services. This model recognizes that information and technology are not separate services, especially in school and academic libraries. By combining these services, this model makes it easier for students to do their research and express their findings in different mediums, such as paper or video. Libraries have partnered with other services to make the information/learning commons a one-stop service for students. Such combinations include writing centers, tutoring programs, advising and counseling services, and a wide range of media technology services. Learning commons can be staffed by a combination of librarians, students, and paraprofessionals who have been trained to assist with the variety of services available. Information/learning commons usually provide access to library resources, productivity software, and scanning, printing, and photocopying equipment. There may also be adaptive technology equipment, video, and film support as well as support for video games and viewing rooms. They often offer students an opportunity to work collaboratively in groups.

At the University of Arizona, an information/learning commons was developed that offered reference assistance in multiple formats. Students could get assistance at the information/learning commons help desk in person; by phone, e-mail, or instant messaging; and by setting up an appointment for an in-depth research consultation. Students were provided with computers and a wide variety of software. The software included was for graphics, web-page creation, statistics, and viewing and listening. The researchers noted that having fewer, permanent staff members made the information/learning commons work better since the staff could become more familiar with the hardware and software. [12] After performing an assessment of questions received at the information/learning commons' reference desk, the library decided that since the majority of reference questions were of the ready reference type, they could best be addressed by the permanent staff trained in dealing with the hardware and software needs of the commons, rather than by other librarians.

Partnerships with other organizations are often utilized when building and instituting an information/learning commons. For example, a report from the Hinckley Library at Northwest College (Wyoming) discussed adding the writing center and the peer tutoring center to the library's learning commons. Each group had their own space, but the spaces were adjacent. Although each group had concerns with balancing the need to address its own organizational goals while promoting a unified front within the information/learning commons, this partnership has been remarkably successful and the use of each service has dramatically increased. [13]

The University of Massachusetts Amherst Library issued a detailed report outlining the aims, planning, development, and implementation of their learning commons. Specifically, the learning commons was developed to address the pedagogical goal outlined by the university of engendering collaborative group work. The placement of technological devices and resources within the learning commons encourages co-located collaborative work, such as by allowing a team to share a particular member's screen. The learning commons also provides a tech support desk to assist students with their projects. The students staffing this desk have been trained to answer basic reference questions and refer more difficult ones. The learning commons is also set up to allow for individual study. Although quantitative measures such as head counts indicate the popularity of the learning commons, the library is constantly trying to determine through surveys and observation how students are using the learning commons, how this use supports their learning outcomes, and what other services and software might be needed to address these outcomes. Additional services, such as a writing center and a café, are also available at the learning commons. [14]

Here are some guidelines for providing an information/learning commons model:

1. Spend time developing a plan and identifying services to offer and groups that might want to partner with the library. These groups could include a writing center or a counseling service.
2. Consider a survey to identify technologies and services needed by the students.
3. Train the staff carefully with frequent refresher sessions.
4. Plan what technology will be provided as well as how the hardware and software will be kept up to date.
5. Be sure it is clear what the information/learning commons provides.
6. Have a code of conduct and computer use policy.
7. Publicize the information/learning commons as a one-stop center where students can get help with their papers and other assignments. Be specific about service hours.
8. Plan periodic assessments.

ROVING/ROAMING REFERENCE

Since we know that many patrons do not approach the reference desk when they have a question, librarians have developed roving reference as a way to meet patron needs. In this book we will always use the term "roving." Roving reference can be defined as the librarian moving around the library and assisting patrons as needed. Roving can be accomplished either by having the staff scheduled to rove during busy hours of the day or by having reference staff members spend part of their time at the reference desk roving. Either way roving needs to be scheduled and not a haphazard activity.

It takes some training to be good at this activity. Librarians need to be able to recognize patrons in need of assistance and develop polite and friendly ways of approaching them. In a 1996 study Eileen Kramer found that roving librarians elicit fewer routine and more in-depth questions than those students bring to the reference desk, further suggesting that just because a service is not being used in one context (e.g., in-depth questions being asked at a reference desk) does not signify that it would not be widely used in another.[15] Roving services tend to be less pervasive in libraries than are information/learning commons and tiered reference services, with Miles indicating in his 2013 study that 47.1 percent of the academic libraries surveyed used roving.[16]

Librarians learned from roving that many reference questions did not reach the reference desk and that roving made them more visible to the patrons. Often more complicated questions are actually identified through roving. They also discovered other patron needs that had not been articulated at the reference desk. The reason roving may elicit more complicated questions may be due to patrons' perceptions of the reference desk as a place to go with a fully articulated research question or even a simple unwillingness to pack up one's things and physically move to the reference desk when in the middle of trying to solve a problem.[17] Kealin McCabe and James Mac-Donald stated that "the simple act of roving has the potential to reinvigorate reference services as a whole, by forcing librarians out of their comfort zones, and allowing them to reach patrons at their point of need."[18] Roving is one of the ways of providing value-added reference service in any kind of library but especially academic and public libraries—both in a computer area and on the floors of the library where there is no reference desk.

One of the ways to meet patrons' needs in the physical library is by roving with a tablet in hand. Libraries have been trying this approach for several years. They have thought that meeting patrons throughout the library and being able to assist them without returning to the reference desk would be a good way to expand service. This has been to some extent successful, but it depended on the development of better tablets and also on the ability of the librarians to be willing to experiment with the tablets to see how this can work. As tablets have gotten lighter, it is, of course, easier to walk around with them. In the meantime, many of the vendors who produce and sell circulation systems have developed interfaces between the systems and tablets so that librarians can check on book availability, check out books, renew, place holds, and even sign up new borrowers. Libraries that are experimenting with tablets include the Boise Public Library and the Hennepin County Library. Boise has replaced PCs for some staff members with tablets and wants their staff members to use them for all their daily functions. Hennepin also uses tablets to show patrons the public catalog and other library functions. These approaches mark just the beginning of how tablets can supplement roving services but will provide new ideas for other libraries that want to provide increased patron services.[19]

In another study at the University of North British Columbia Library, the library decided to start a roving reference service combined with their chat service to increase usage. The librarians felt that roving reference would make the reference service more visible and provide more immediate assistance to the patron. The roving shift lasted ninety minutes during which the librarians could periodically return to their desks and then go out on another roam. If the student contacting the librarian via the chat service was in the library, the librarian would offer to come to the student. Otherwise the librarian would answer the question virtually. Statistics assessing implementation of these services showed some interesting results—63 percent of the roving questions in fall 2010 were research ones. Many questions (51 percent) could be answered in one to five minutes; however, a significant number of questions were more in depth (49 percent). Thirty-five percent of the transactions occurred on the first floor of the library where the reference desk was located, suggesting that perhaps patrons do not want to interrupt their more in-depth research work to physically visit the reference desk, although further study is required to address this observation. In regard to the medium, 46 percent of the questions were answered by chat and 31 percent by roving. The next semester, the library decided to integrate traditional reference service with roving, which was not successful because librarians were too busy at the reference desk to rove. In addition, the iPad roving software being used turned out to lack many of the key features essential to its successful implementation. The study concluded that "all a roving reference service needs to be a success is staff members who are willing to roam and any mobile devise that can tell them where to go."[20]

A study of roving reference at the University of Mississippi found that 42 percent of questions were reference based with the others pertaining to needed printing and copying assistance, among other miscellaneous needs. Of the reference questions, 56 percent were "locational questions about known, specific library materials—needing detailed assistance and with additional questions," 22 percent were "locational questions about a type of library material—needing detailed research assistance at a library location," and 22 percent were "research questions needing a comprehensive answer—not location-based."[21] Of key importance was the fact that the author of the study, Ruth M. Mirtz, found that all of these question types represented the second stage for students, who had already asked questions at the reference desk but were now in the process of locating their materials. In other words, when they submitted a roving reference question, they had moved from the reference desk to another part of the library and now they needed more assistance and still had questions. Mirtz called it "the second half of reference."[22] So the roving was needed to provide additional assistance often at a specific location—the point of need.

Here are some guidelines for setting up a roving service:

1. Have an agreed-upon definition of what roving is and what is expected of the librarian roving.
2. Provide some training to staff as to how to approach patrons and what services they should be providing. Customer-service training is especially useful.
3. Discuss how referrals are to be done.
4. Have a schedule for roving. It might be part of the duties at the reference desk.
5. Keep statistics on the number of patrons assisted while roving.
6. Include a question about the patrons' responses to roving on library surveys.

COMBINING POINTS OF SERVICE

One way to be more efficient in a library while providing good reference service is to combine points of service. For example, some libraries have combined circulation and reference services into one unit. They may refer to these services as "concierge" services since the patron can receive personalized services that are not limited to one particular service.

Beverly Murphy and colleagues documented the careful change to a single service point at the Duke University Medical Center Library and Archives.[23] The work to move to a single service point began in 1998 and continued to 2006 and beyond. It began with a task force looking at patron convenience and efficient use of staff. Over time new task forces were set up to move forward. Staff members were involved in all the decision making. One issue they focused on was the importance of communication and how this would affect the delivery of the library's services. Basic competencies of the staff were outlined with the emphasis on staff training as the basic functions of circulation and reference were combined. In 2005 an "on-call reference" pilot project was begun with librarians working reference hours from their offices. A new manual was developed and posted to the library intranet in 2006. In order to improve training, it was changed from annual to quarterly. The need to continue to evaluate service desk core competencies as changes in library service occurred was noted.[24]

In another study the Kansas State University Library decided to consolidate eight of its nine service points into one service point, the circulation desk, based on the results of a LibQUAL survey and focus group. For a number of reasons this model proved unworkable. The desk itself was a disadvantage since, like many circulation desks, it was wide (four feet wide) so that the staff members behind the desk were far from the patrons. Further, the desk did not have a monitor facing the patrons. Both features contributed to the creation of visual cues indicating that the librarians at the circulation desk were not to be interacted with by patrons. In addition, because so many desks had been consolidated (i.e., information, reference, science reference, government documents, interlibrary loan [ILL], and reserves), staff members complained they had too much to learn to provide a single point of service. In general, the librarians found that with this new arrangement they had less ability to provide quality service. As a result of this change, reference statistics dropped considerably.

To address these issues, the library added a reference desk near the circulation desk, which could provide more personalized service. This implementation proved successful, and reference statistics increased. In both instances detailed here, combining different points of service must be consistently evaluated for effectiveness by the staff (e.g., internal communication, training, and satisfaction) and patrons (e.g., whether the service is visible and approachable).[25]

As a subset of combining points of service, many libraries have developed what they call a "triage" model for reference services. This model provides one point of service for all reference questions but then the questions can be referred as needed, either to a nonprofessional staff member or to a reference librarian depending on the question. Similar to findings regarding the implementation of reference desk staffing, offering a new means through which to access different types of reference services appears to be a more efficient way to handle information inquiries than relying on librarians alone.

At the University Libraries at Grand Valley State University researchers studied the results of traditional reference service versus a single point-of-service model: a virtual reference service. The library used various patterns of staffing to better understand differences between staffing the reference desk and providing on-call service. These patterns included semesters with alternate weeks of reference desk staffing and on-call staffing, only reference desk staffing, and only on-call staffing. Statistics were kept by question categories, such as directional, ready reference, strategy-based searching (reference), and citation formatting. The statistics indicated that "the number of true reference questions . . . answered by librarians remained almost the same. . . . So while the higher-level reference questions and citation related questions are being answered by librarians, whether they are staffing a reference desk or are on call, the other questions are no longer coming to the librarians."[26] This strategic focus on assigning the best staffer for a given service is also exemplified by Julie Garrison, from Grand Valley State University Libraries, who wrote in another article about how the Grand Valley State University Library activated partnerships with other university partners to offer students peer writing assistance, presentation help, and research strategies within their "Knowledge Market."[27]

Other examples of successful combinations of single points of service include the University of Virginia Claude Moore Health Sciences Library, University of Virginia Health Services, which closed its reference desk after the library developed a triage system wherein a single service desk, located at the circulation desk, could forward questions through LibraryH3lp, a chat platform, to reference staff. Patrons could then chat with a reference librarian to get needed assistance. Questions not requiring a reference librarian were handled by service desk staff. In this library, reference staff has found it necessary to maintain a schedule so that staff members will be available at all times to answer questions.

A final example is the University of Connecticut Library, which changed its reference services when the staff realized the students worked in ways not captured by current services. Specifically, students wanted to work on their own but have the staff available to help when needed. As a result, staff combined services into two desks: an iDesk, which includes information services, circulation, reserves, and ILL pickup, and a learning commons help desk. Each desk is staffed by a mix of librarians and students. The library also provides an on-call reference service, a research consultation service, and a virtual help service for those who communicate by e-mail, chat, or text messaging. Scott Kennedy, in describing this new way of providing reference assistance, called it "distributed reference services" and said they are "presenting the library as a platform for 'getting academic projects done' providing appropriate tools and stepping aside."[28]

CONCLUSION

The changes in reference service described in this chapter are the first major steps to change the way we handle reference service and serve the patron. They acknowledge that there is more to reference service than just the reference desk; that not all patrons are comfortable asking their questions at the reference desk; and that having services so separate wastes the time of the patron. Tiered reference expands for both the patron and the librarian the difference between a ready reference question and a reference question. Roving reference is another way of working with patrons who for many reasons don't approach the reference desk. In this case the librarian comes to the patron instead of the patron coming to the librarian. Single-point service saves the patrons time by allowing them to accomplish more than one task at the same desk. And finally, the learning commons provides more services for the patron who can possibly complete a whole project in one place. These changes begin to move reference in new directions as they recognize new patron needs.

Table 2.1. Advantages, disadvantages, and ideal situations for use of various reference types

Reference type	Advantages	Disadvantages	Ideal situations for use
Desk	Provides patrons with human contact. Symbolizes reference service.	Not all users come to the desk for assistance. Not anonymous. May not be the best use of the librarian's time since many questions could be answered by a paraprofessional.	As a single point of service. In tiered reference situations.
Tiered	Provides users with a range of services. Makes most efficient use of librarian's skills.	May not provide appropriate reference referrals. Requires increased training and evaluation.	Provides ready reference in tandem with consultation services provided by librarians.
Roving	Addresses patrons at their point of need. Increases visibility of reference services.	Librarians may be too busy at the reference desk to be able to rove. Requires additional scheduling, training, and evaluation.	To address more in-depth reference questions. In academic and public libraries, especially in the computer area.
Consultation	Increases the library experience. Can be scheduled in advance.	Requires additional time of trained professionals.	In tandem with tiered reference models.
Information/learning commons	Incorporates related services, such as writing centers and adaptive technology.	Requires increased training and evaluation.	In situations where a small number of permanent staff members can be trained to support its software and hardware.
Combined points of service	Increases visibility of reference services. Pairs an information need with the best staffer available to address it.	Requires continual evaluation. Requires increased training.	Useful when integrated with a triage model of reference services.

NOTES

1. Barbara J. Ford, "Reference Beyond (and Without) the Reference Desk," *College and Research Libraries* 47, no. 5 (1986): 491–94; Steven J. Bell, "Who Needs a Reference Desk?" *Library Issues: Briefings for Faculty and Administrators* 27, no. 6 (2007): 1–4; Keith Ewing and Robert Hauptman, "Is Traditional Reference Services Obsolete?" *Journal of Academic Librarianship* 21, no. 1 (1995): 3–6; Karen S. Summerhill, "The High Cost of Reference: The Need to Reassess Services and Service Delivery," *Reference Librarian* 20, no. 43 (1994): 71–85.

2. Karen Sobel, "Promoting Library Reference Services to First-Year Undergraduate Students: What Works?" *Reference and User Services Quarterly* 48, no. 4 (2009): 369.

3. Dennis B. Miles, "Shall We Get Rid of the Reference Desk?" *Reference and Patron Services Quarterly* 52, no. 4 (2013): 320.

4. Ibid., 323–24.

5. Ibid., 321.

6. Virginia Massey-Burzio, "Reference Encounter of a Different Kind: A Symposium," *Journal of Academic Librarianship* 18, no. 5 (1992): 276–81.

7. Thelma Freides, "Current Trends in Academic Libraries," *Library Trends* 31, no. 3 (1983): 457–74.

8. Christy R. Stevens, "Reference Reviewed and Re-envisioned: Revamping Librarian and Desk-Centric Services with LibStARs and LibAnswers," *Journal of Academic Librarianship* 39, no. 2 (2013): 209.

9. Ibid., 202–14.

10. Pixey A. Mosley, "Assessing Patron Interactions at the Desk Nearest the Front Door," *Reference and User Services Quarterly* 42, no. 2 (2007): 159–67.

11. Miles, "Shall We Get Rid?" 327.

12. Carla J. Stoffle and Cheryl Cuillier, "Student-Centered Services and Support: A Case Study of the University of Arizona Libraries' Information Commons," *Journal of Library Administration* 50, no. 2 (2010): 117–34.

13. Renee Dechert et al., "Exploring the Learning Commons," *College and Research Libraries News* 75, no. 3 (2014): 125–46.

14. Sarah C. Hutton, Robert C. Davis, and Carol Will, "Term-Based Ingenuity Supporting 21st Century Learners," *Collaborative Librarianship* 4, no. 4 (2012): 149–64.

15. Eileen H. Kramer, "Why Roving Reference: A Case Study in a Small Academic Library," *Reference Services Review* 24, no. 3 (1996): 67–80.

16. Miles, "Shall We Get Rid?"

17. Kealin M. McCabe and James R. W. MacDonald, "Roaming Reference: Reinvigorating Reference through Point of Need Service," *Partnership: The Canadian Journal of Library and Information Practice and Research* 6, no. 2 (2011), https://journal.lib.uoguelph.ca/.

18. Ibid.

19. Matt Enis, "Meet the Tabletarians," *Library Journal* 140, no. 1 (2014): 39–41.

20. McCabe and MacDonald, "Roaming Reference."

21. Ruth M. Mirtz, "The Second Half of Reference: An Analysis of Point-of-Need Roving Reference Questions," in *Association of College and Research Libraries 2013 Proceedings* (Chicago: American Library Association, 2013), 520.

22. Ibid., 518.

23. Beverly Murphy et al., "Revolution at the Library Service Desk," *Medical Reference Services Quarterly* 27, no. 4 (2008): 379–93.

24. Ibid.

25. Melia E. Fritch, Laura Bonella, and Jason Coleman, "Nothing Is Permanent but Change: The Journey to Consolidation and Back," *College and Undergraduate Libraries* 21, no. 1 (2014): 2–18.

26. Patricia Bravender and Hazel McClure, "Regarding Reference in an Academic Library: Does the Desk Make a Difference?" *Reference and Patron Services Quarterly* 52, no. 4 (2013): 306–7.

27. Julie Garrison, "What Do We Do Now? A Case for Abandoning Yesterday and Making the Future," *Reference and User Services Quarterly (RUSQ)* 51, no. 1 (2011): 12.

28. Scott Kennedy, "Farewell to the Reference Librarian," *Journal of Library Administration* 51, no. 4 (2011): 324–25.

Chapter Three

Identifying New Ways of Providing Reference Services and Communicating with Users

Reference services are changing as librarians realize they must reach patrons where they are. Not all patrons want or can come to a physical library. Many barriers stand in the way of people using libraries, such as distance, cost, time, or disability. Further, patrons may not choose to use reference services unless they can articulate an information need. Yet that does not mean that people do not want to use libraries. The Pew Research Center's Internet and American Life Project report in January 2013 stated that "80 percent (of their respondents) say reference librarians are a 'very important' service of libraries."[1]

Librarians have been and continue to explore ways to meet their patrons' identified and unidentified information needs. Ways of reaching patrons beyond the physical walls of the library include e-mail, chat reference, text messaging, Facebook, Twitter, and Skype. What began as extra services have slowly become integrated into reference services. Such integration can mean that the contact between librarian and patron begins one way but then changes over time depending on the needs of the patron. For example, the first contact made by a patron might be via text message, followed by an e-mail or an actual face-to-face library visit. As this new face of library service develops, libraries can expand their patron base to serve an even broader audience.

This chapter explores reference services that go beyond the walls of the library. It discusses how librarians are reaching patrons who do not come into the library but are in need of library services. Many libraries are trying new

Figure 3.1.   The new look of the reference desk prepared for new ways of communicating with patrons.

services and studying the results to see what actually works and how they can improve services provided to their patrons.

VIRTUAL REFERENCE

Virtual reference has grown slowly, as libraries have adopted and marketed it to their patrons. It includes e-mail, chat, text messaging, instant messaging, Facebook, Skype, and Twitter. Recent statistics indicated that 55 percent of libraries and 85 percent of library websites offer some form of virtual reference.[2] Types of virtual reference services can be divided into two categories: synchronous services that operate in real time and include instant messaging, text messaging, Skype and chat, and asynchronous services that require the patron to wait for a response, such as e-mail and Facebook. Convenience proves to be a significant factor among patrons when assessing virtual reference services.[3] While a significant advantage to asynchronous reference services is that librarians have more time to pull together resources to answer the question, patrons may not want to wait for an indefinite amount of time for a response to their e-mail request when they can instantly talk to a reference librarian using the chat service. Therefore, synchronous reference services are important since they can respond to a patron at the point of need.

More libraries are also trying to provide 24/7 virtual reference services by partnering with other libraries to coordinate centralized service provision. An example of such a service is AskUsNow! Maryland (http://askusnow.info/), which represents a collaboration between partner libraries within the state and is made available to in-state residents. Although there are not many questions asked at certain hours, the fact that the library service is always available promotes its use. Through May 2016, AskUsNow! Maryland has received 457,000 questions by chat and over 127,000 questions by e-mail and follow-up (http://askusnow.info/about).

Many studies have been conducted on virtual reference services in recent years. Topics of study include types of channels used (e.g., chat, text, and video), case studies of service implementation, and the general web presence of libraries. In regard to channel types, a study conducted from a random sample of 362 institutions listed on Peterson's Four Year Colleges 2013 found that 47.5 percent of college libraries provide chat reference—only 16 percent of these libraries have a chat widget on the main page of the library's website. The other 31 percent of libraries have the widget on a subpage. Placing the widget on a subpage does not necessarily indicate a lack of visibility for the service, however, given that the library may provide a button advertising the service on the home page. Other findings of interest indicated that the likelihood of a library offering chat services was influenced by the size of the undergraduate student body (the larger, the more likely), if graduate degrees are offered, and finally, if the institution is public.[4]

Compared to chat services, a larger number of college libraries offered e-mail (65 percent) and telephone reference (69 percent). The fact that more libraries provide these services could be for several reasons, including lower cost of service delivery and longer permanence of e-mail and telephone-based technologies. Future research will be needed to map the adoption of more recent technologies, such as chat and text messaging, to determine whether they will ultimately supersede, be used in conjunction with, or be less used than e-mail and telephone. For the time being, it appears that use of multiple channels for reference service provision seems most popular, with the same study indicating that the majority of libraries offered two to four types of reference services: e-mail, telephone, text, or chat.[5]

Anthony Chow and Rebecca Croxton performed a usability study to see which forms of virtual reference students preferred and whether there was any difference based on the type of question asked and the age, gender, or race of the patron. This study emphasized the usability of virtual reference services including e-mail, telephone, chat, text messaging, and Skype. Participants, who tended to be nonusers of reference services, were asked to use each type of service to answer a factual question and a research question. For both question types, the patrons rated the online chat the highest in effectiveness, efficiency, and satisfaction. The telephone was rated second; and e-mail, third. These ratings held constant regardless of age, gender, or race. To explicate their choice of sources, the patrons in the study said that online chat combines the immediacy of the phone, the convenience of the written record, the content sharing of e-mail, and the immediacy of text messaging and Skype. The authors noted that these results reflect that students often engage in satisfying behaviors, and also suggested that the popularity of text messaging may change patrons' priorities in the future based on their increasing use and comfort with this technology.[6]

Case studies of implementation include an article by Erica Nicol and Linda Crook, about the development of virtual reference services at Washington State University, Pullman. In 2012, the library decided to move the virtual reference services, which included e-mail, LibAnswers, instant messaging, and text messaging, to a more unified model. To this end, the library combined these services within the LibAnswers platform, which gave the library a knowledge base that answers frequently asked questions, as well as chat and text message questions, and fostered collaboration among reference librarians. Virtual reference services were separated from face-to-face reference, which ameliorated previous issues of emphasizing one service type over the other. The most successful part of this implementation was the chat service, where usage increased significantly. The authors state that marketing plus better tools and support, and extended hours, were all responsible for the increased use of chat.[7]

Finally, an example of a study focusing on the web presence of libraries, in regard to both websites and social media, was performed by Linda Hofschire and Meghan Wanucha, who found that most public libraries have a web presence. However, the type of web presence differed by size, with larger libraries more likely to have mobile-friendly website access. This finding has importance when considering that certain groups of individuals report solely accessing the Internet via their mobile phones, in particular those with lower incomes and educational attainment levels, younger adults, and nonwhites.[8] Additional findings found that the majority of public libraries had at least one social media account, with the largest public libraries having about 3.5 social networks, and were most likely to be on Facebook and Twitter. Again, these findings could be interpreted in the sense that specific groups of people use Facebook and Twitter, and raises questions as to whether libraries should select the most popular social media sites to use or survey the needs of the community by asking about its social media use. Public libraries reported employing social media to promote their services, materials, and events. They also used it to tell patrons the good things they were doing, such as offering homework help sessions. Contests were often held to raise patrons' awareness of the library's web presence. Some libraries cleverly tied together in-person and online events, such as the New York Public Library offering Google Hangouts that allow virtual participation, as well as contests beginning online and culminating in physical displays and activities taking place at the library.[9]

CHAT REFERENCE

Many libraries have moved to chat reference using a number of software packages. These include LibraryH31p, Altamara, Mosio, and LibAnswers. Chat is a very effective form of virtual reference because it offers the opportunity for librarians to do a reference interview and be sure they understand the patron's question. It also allows the library to send links to the patron, which can then be evaluated for their usefulness, and follow up with a transcript. Although originally many thought that patrons using chat needed a very quick response, it is now understood that the patron may be willing to spend some time on the chat. Many chats last longer. Chat also provides the opportunity for some personalized instructional services. Librarians often take time to discuss such things as database searching, search strategies, and online resources. Because patrons often go to chat when they are engaged in a project, it can be just the right moment for librarians to provide them with information on library resources and accommodate patrons who may not have a clearly articulated information need. Libraries have also experimented with more abbreviated forms of virtual reference such as instant messaging (IM), texting, and tweeting. These are ways to communicate if a long response is not needed and are particularly good for frequently asked and ready reference questions. Those using these abbreviated forms of virtual reference may be directed to other formats or to the library itself if the information they need is more extensive.

A most interesting, recent study of chat reference is by Krisellen Maloney and Jan Kemp. In this study, the University of Texas library system believed that many students had more complex research questions despite the low number of questions being asked within the library's reference services. To address this issue and make virtual reference central to the students in the way it is central by use of a physical reference desk, the library installed a new chat system that put a chat box on all pages of the library website. As a result of this placement, the rate of chat questions asked per day went from seven to forty-three in a month. The next month, the rate of questions asked increased to 444 per day, with further increases in the months to follow.[10]

The researchers also asked whether the number of complex reference questions had increased and if the questions were more complex on chat than at the reference desk. By dividing the questions into ones nonprofessionals, generalists, or librarians could answer, the authors found that 25 percent of the chat questions were more complex than could be addressed by a paraprofessional and thus required a librarian. This finding represented a higher number of complex questions than found in previous studies. The researchers attributed this increase to the fact that the patron could ask a question at the point of need, which represented an important affordance provided by chat-based services. In other words, the librarians realized from the kind of questions asked online due to the new proactive chat that more patrons required librarian assistance than what was previously indicated. So whereas many have thought that a librarian is not necessarily needed for chat reference, this study indicated the opposite. These findings also made the authors question the efficacy of a tiered reference model for virtual reference, given the high number of complex questions being asked via proactive chat.[11]

A similar study was conducted by Jie Zhang and Nevin Mayer at John Carroll University. They decided to use Zopim, a business-oriented software for chat. There was a live-chat widget on each web page that could initiate a chat. If the patron was on a web page for more than three minutes, Zopim automatically initiated a chat. If the patron responded, a librarian would then take over the chat. The authors found that with the software-initiated chat, there were more reference and research questions (74 percent) than when patrons initiated the chat (57 percent). This finding indicated that there are many questions patrons may have that go unanswered when it is expected by librarians that patrons initiate the chat.[12]

Another important element of developing chat reference is how it should be implemented in relation to face-to-face reference. This issue was discussed by Vicky Duncan and Angie Gerrard from the University of Saskatchewan. Their survey of virtual reference patrons revealed that 30 percent had never used the face-to-face services, indicating that the virtual reference services were, in fact, reaching new patrons. The librarians discussed the need to integrate the chat reference service with the face-to-face one to provide equity of access to all patrons regardless of which service they used. Over the next few years the two reference services were merged so that they have equal priority and receive the same number of hours of service. In this way patrons receive equal service and content is not judged or valued differently by librarians depending on which platform it is shared. The findings therefore suggest that librarians cannot necessarily predict that the type of content shared via chat channels is less complex than that exchanged face-to-face. Instead other factors, such as convenience of access and visibility of the service, may influence certain question types being exchanged over others.[13]

Stephen Francoeur, writing about digital reference services, emphasized the importance of the patron experience. Here are some of his recommendations:

1. The way the services are labeled on the library's website is important to the patrons' ability to locate what they need.

Figure 3.2.   Live chat is an important way to communicate with users.

2. Providing access to services in more than one place on the website makes the services easier to find.
3. Think strategically about where on the library website the patron might be having trouble and needing assistance.
4. Do not use the same words to describe more than one service. It will be confusing to the patron.

5. Try to keep the forms patrons have to fill out for virtual reference services as simple as possible.
6. Develop subject guides and other pieces of instructional learning that can be used to assist the patron.
7. Try usability testing to see if the library's language used on the website and how it is organized make sense to the patron.[14]

TEXT MESSAGING OR TEXTING

Texting is a newer form of communication and is used to convey short messages. Libraries have been running text-messaging reference services since about 2005.[15] Texting is most popular with the younger generation, who use devices such as smartphones to text.[16] According to the Pew Research Center (2015), about 68 percent of all American adults and 86 percent of all young adults own a smartphone.[17] As texting becomes more widespread, there may be a concordant increase in virtual reference services using this medium. Currently, libraries can run a text-messaging service using a cell phone or smartphone dedicated to this service or a commercial service such as RefChatter (http://www.altarama.com), Mosio for Libraries (http://www.textalibrarian.com), or LibraryH3lp (https://libraryh3lp.com/).

Lili Luo surveyed patrons of public libraries in 2013 and found that only 15.8 percent used texting. The majority of these patrons were between the ages of eighteen and forty. Of this group only 22.9 percent had used the texting service several times. Those using the service liked it because it was easy to use, convenient, and fast, and it provided reliable information. Of libraries that offered the texting service, the survey indicated that nonusers were often not aware of it, which indicated a need to promote it. Those who reported using the service only a few times may have done so due to the fact that, as reported by responses to other survey items, they did not know how to use it and what kind of questions to ask. Steps that a library could take to promote this texting service could be to display it prominently on the library website and market it to patrons who have the demographic characteristics of those who text.[18]

In regard to the context type, an earlier study by Luo and Emily Weak indicated that 70 percent of text questions were ready reference. These questions asked for factual and statistical information, information about people, information about places and addresses, and local library information such as policies and procedures. These findings suggest that unlike chat, text-based reference content may not include more complex questions, although further research is needed to confirm these findings.[19]

In regard to the efficacy and efficiency of texting services, the library at Sam Houston State University in Huntsville, Texas, has offered a texting service since January 2010 using Mosio's Text a Librarian (now Mosio for Libraries). In their three-year study of this service, Erin Dorris Cassidy, Angela Colmenares, and Michelle Martinez found that 59 percent of the text messages sent by patrons were responded to by librarians in thirty minutes or less, with 51 percent responded to in ten minutes.[20]

This response time cannot be evaluated without considering patron expectations and question types, among other factors. To this end, the authors further evaluated the questions using the Reference and User Services Association's (RUSA) "Guidelines for Behavioral Performance of Reference and Information Service Providers."[21] These guidelines consisted of the following factors: listening and inquiry, interest, searching, and follow-up. Questions received the lowest scores in follow-up and listening and inquiry. These skills both focus on librarian communication skills and indicate that librarians must derive accommodations for communication cues lost by using a text-based platform. For example, a librarian cannot indicate active listening to a patron via text. Librarians can communicate some of these lost cues by sending texts to the patron indicating that they are actively working on the request, among other strategies. Based on these findings, the library planned to do follow-up training to improve these communication skills and increase the 19 percent of patrons who indicated that they were repeat customers of the texting service.

Another study of the use of text-based reference services was completed by Kimberly Vardeman and Ian Barba at Texas Tech University, which added text messaging to its virtual reference services in 2011 using Mosio for Libraries. The library's study covers data from three years of use. It found that students used text messaging mostly between 1:00 a.m. and 6:00 p.m. with half of the texts received on Wednesday. The questions were quite short—an average character count of 60.9. The median response time was 7.1 minutes, but the response time was slower between 10:00 p.m. and 5:00 a.m. and on weekends. The question types were similar to those within chat and face-to-face modalities—37 percent reference, 17 percent directional, 14 percent equipment, and 10 percent circulation. The study authors noted that use of the texting service had declined each year since it started, except for a spike in 2011 when the library marketed the service. During this same period, use of the chat service stayed constant, while use of e-mail service increased. The authors speculated that perhaps the students preferred chat rather than texting since chat is synchronous and they may have to wait for a response when texting. The authors also noted that the lack of marketing for the texting service might have contributed to its low use. However, similar to Maloney and Kemp,[22] and Duncan and Gerrard's studies,[23] Vardeman and Barba still thought that texting served a purpose in their suite of virtual reference services.[24]

Below are some recommended guidelines for a texting service:

1. Identify how the texting will be done using a cell phone, smartphone, or texting software, and develop a plan or strategy for the texting service.
2. Train staff members how to handle this service, and indicate what they can accomplish using texting.
3. Set response time goals that can usually be met.
4. Staff the service so that patrons will get reasonably quick responses.
5. Survey the patrons to find out more about their satisfaction with and expectations of the service.
6. Continue to promote the texting service through the library website, social-networking sites, and so forth.

TWITTER

Twitter is another useful way to reach patrons and has the potential to develop community relationships and engender patron engagement. Twitter acts as a way to provide short updates and announcements or to start a conversation. With similar constraints to text-based communication, the patron can post up to 140 characters in each post including spaces. Tweets from public accounts are visible to anyone viewing the Twitter profile page. Twitter users can also follow content posted by others.

Although Twitter represents a popular social media service, with over 310 million active patrons as of March 2016,[25] libraries need to plan their institutional face on Twitter before they begin to use the platform. Including a photo of the library or a link to the library's website on the library's Twitter profile is recommended. Use of library images will create credibility and encourage patrons to follow the library and use its services. Once the library has decided to use Twitter, it is important for the library to stay engaged on the site and have a staff member who checks it regularly. Sporadic Twitter use will probably not bring the library much success on the platform.[26]

Some of the ways that librarians have been using Twitter are as follows:

1. Providing quick updates about library hours, events, and programming as well as spotlighting new library resources
2. Sharing links to LibGuides and answering ready reference questions
3. Using search alerts to proactively notify the library if people are using certain words such as "research," "paper," or "reading." The search proximity feature allows the library to bound these alerts to tweets within the immediate geographic area. The library can then reach out to those people and respond if it seems appropriate.
4. Tweeting information about the library and retweeting relevant information

5. Partnering with other organizations to retweet their messages in exchange for retweeting the library's messages

More specific use of Twitter can be divided by type of library. Public libraries generally use Twitter to tweet upcoming programs and events, let patrons know about changes in operating hours, and highlight items on the library's website. In contrast, academic libraries tweet about services, upcoming events, and instruction workshops, while special libraries can share information about resources and services within their organization.

A few examples of how academic libraries are using Twitter are as follows: Yale University Libraries use Twitter to announce workshops on library resources and provide links to online archives, MIT Libraries provide information on workshop classes and study group information, and the University of British Columbia Libraries tweet reference questions that give patrons an idea of the kind of research the libraries are doing.[27]

Although we think of Twitter as a means to reach patrons, it can also assist the librarian in answering reference questions. A strategically developed network of librarians on Twitter can assist in answering difficult, subject-based questions by leveraging one another's specializations and crowdsourcing answers. Courtney Young provided an example of a public exchange on Twitter between two librarians in which the first has completed a reference interview and posted the portion of the reference question she needed help with to a law librarian with the requisite expertise. The law librarian then tweeted back the relevant information to the first librarian, who could then provide the resource to her patron. In this way, Twitter provides a synchronous means to share knowledge among librarians that can be very productive and efficient within a reference environment.[28]

Twitter has a Help Center (https://support.twitter.com) for those needing assistance with any aspect of Twitter.

Based on the previous discussion, recommended guidelines for using Twitter are as follows:

1. Plan how the library will use Twitter.
2. Make sure to have a picture or link on Twitter to the library's website to enhance credibility.
3. Make sure that the library's Twitter account matches its other branding.
4. Consider creating a network of colleagues for tweeting and retweeting.[29]

FACEBOOK

Facebook can enhance a library's image and visibility by allowing patrons to either "friend" or "follow" the library for information. Libraries use Facebook for several reasons, including community building and providing links to library resources. Libraries can also promote events and services on Facebook. Unlike Twitter, Facebook is often used for responding to reference questions.

Scott Stone, the performing arts librarian at Chapman University, discussed using his personal Facebook account to friend students and faculty. He had read in the library literature that students and faculty did not use library reference services because this encounter made them anxious. The literature pointed out that if patrons got to know a librarian on a more personal level they were more apt to approach him or her with reference questions. Stone's experience proved this finding to be true. Although most of the reference questions from students did not come through Facebook, students who knew Stone through his Facebook page used face-to-face reference services more often. On the other hand, faculty used virtual services more often, which was understandable since many were adjunct faculty and therefore might not be on campus and have access to physical library resources.[30]

Recommended guidelines for Facebook are as follows:

1. Plan the library's Facebook page carefully.
2. Use the library's Facebook page to link to library resources such as the catalog and LibGuides.
3. Promote events and library services on Facebook.
4. Be open to answering reference questions on Facebook. This openness means monitoring the site with some frequency.

MOBILE SERVICES

Mobile services are now coming into their own as more patrons have smartphones and can use them for seeking and finding information, as indicated by the statistics provided in the "Text Messaging or Texting" section of this chapter. Mobile devices are most often used for accessing the local catalog or WorldCat and databases that have a mobile platform. New technology makes it possible to design websites that adapt to the device used to access them. As patrons have come to depend on their smartphones for everything, patrons want to be able to access library information using smartphones too. The study performed by Hofschire and Wanucha on libraries' web use indicates a gap between libraries that offer access to their websites and services on mobile platforms and those that do not. But the gap is beginning to close. By

Table 3.1.

	Questions addressed	Context of use	Expectations of use
Email	Many in-depth reference questions	In situations where libraries are limited in the number of staff available to respond	Generates a written record Content sharing Gives the librarian time to do a thorough job
Chat	In-depth reference questions, such as those that are project based	Can conduct reference interviews Can provide instruction	Convenient Synchronous At point of need
Text messaging	Ready-reference questions	For users who may just have access to the Internet via their mobile phones Younger users	Convenient Instant
Skype	Can have a conversation	For people who cannot physically access the library	Instant
Twitter	Ready-reference questions	To market library services and events	Convenient Instant
Facebook	Marketing and less used for reference questions	To market library services and events To "friend" students and faculty, and make them comfortable to pursue face-to-face reference services	Convenient Familiarity with library staff

2012, three-quarters of the largest libraries surveyed had a mobile-friendly website, and three-fifths of the libraries between 25,000 and 499,999 had one. This gap will need to be bridged to accommodate patron demand, provided the library has individuals with the technical resources to adapt these websites for mobile use.[31]

Some studies have explored the demand for mobile reference services. A study performed by Paula Barnett-Ellis and Charlcie Pettway Vann at Jacksonville State University found that patrons expressed a need for more mobile access to library services. Specifically, the students, rather than faculty and staff, indicated that they would find mobile access convenient for virtual reference, the online catalog, and periodical databases. However, a gap existed between the 35.4 percent of students surveyed that used virtual reference services and the 54 percent who used mobile devices for academic work. The authors noted that this gap could be addressed by better marketing the library's resources, specifically their mobile reference services, of which students seemed to be unaware.[32] Another survey by William Caniano and Amy Catalano at Hofstra University found that 50 percent of the students reported using their mobile device to access the library, predominately to use research databases (44 percent). In addition, 27 percent accessed their public library website using mobile devices, indicating that use of mobile services is not just limited to within academic libraries. Graduate students accessed the library from mobile devices more often than undergraduates and favored reading short articles (up to five pages) from their mobile devices. However, patrons reported difficulty accessing the library catalog on their mobile devices, suggesting that the usability of the current service could be improved. In conclusion, the authors stated that "the 'mobile device' is becoming the primary gateway to the Internet and, thus the library," and for this reason, libraries need to better understand both who is using mobile services and their ease of use.[33]

As mobile device technology advances and more people use it, libraries must increase mobile access to reference services. Patron surveys will help libraries decide what their next steps pertaining to implementation of this access should be. Offering subject guides such as LibGuides and other online guidance tools could be very useful, as well as other forms of library instruction and personalized learning opportunities.

Some guidelines to consider for mobile access include the following:

1. Survey patrons as to how they use their mobile phones.
2. Find out what information library patrons want to access on their phones.
3. Have a website designed for mobile access.
4. Plan to expand mobile access to the library's resources as usage grows.

CONCLUSION

While use of both social media and other digital services has increased among patrons, libraries cannot simply adopt these technologies for technology's sake. As indicated by the research presented in this chapter, adding virtual reference services requires planning on the part of the library. A process needs to be developed by the library that specifies how the service will work, both individually and in relation to other reference services. Decisions also need to be made as to how face-to-face and virtual reference services will be staffed, including hours and guidelines. The library must make decisions about virtual reference services based on its patron population and available resources—human, information, and financial.[34] Implementing virtual reference services also requires a communications plan. Most importantly, the library needs to decide which media it will use to provide virtual reference services. Too many different media at one time can make it impossible for both librarians and patrons to keep up. So implementation of virtual reference services is better using one or two mediums well, particularly those already used by the community or communities that the library serves.

NOTES

1. Kathryn Zickuhr, Lee Rainie, and Kristen Purcell, "Library Services in the Digital Age," report, Pew Research Center's Internet and American Life Project, Washington, DC, 2013, http://libraries.pewinternet.org/.

2. Anthony S. Chow and Rebecca A. Croxton, "A Usability Evaluation of Academic Virtual Reference Services," *College and Research Libraries* 75, no. 3 (2014): 309–61.

3. Marie L. Radford and Lynn Silipigni Connaway, "Seeking Synchronicity: Evaluating Virtual Reference Services from Patron, Non-Patron and Librarian Perspectives," report, OCLC, Dublin, OH, 2008, http://www.oclc.org/.

4. Sharon Q. Yang and Heather A. Dalal, "Delivering Virtual Reference Services on the Web: An Investigation into the Current Practice by Academic Libraries," *Journal of Academic Librarianship* 41, no. 1 (2015): 68–86.

5. Ibid.

6. Chow and Croxton, "Usability Evaluation."

7. Erica C. Nicol and Linda Crook, "Now It's Necessary: Virtual Reference Services at Washington State University, Pullman," *Journal of Academic Librarianship* 39, no. 2 (2013): 161–68.

8. "The Smartphone Difference," report, Pew Research Center, Washington, DC, 2015, http://www.pewinternet.org/.

9. Linda Hofschire and Meghan Wanucha, "Public Library Websites and Social Media: What's #Trending Now?" *Computers in Libraries* 34, no. 8 (2014): 4–9.

10. Krisellen Maloney and Jan H. Kemp, "Changes in Reference Question Complexity Following the Implementation of a Proactive Chat System: Implications for Practice," *College and Research Libraries* 74, no. 6 (2015): 959–74.

11. Ibid.

12. Jie Zhang and Nevin Mayer, "Proactive Chat Reference: Getting in the Users' Space," *College and Research Libraries News* 75, no. 4 (2014): 202–5.

13. Vicky Duncan and Angie Gerrard, "All Together Now! Integrating Virtual Reference in the Academic Library," *Reference and Patron Services Quarterly* 50, no. 3 (2011): 280–92.

14. Stephen Francoeur, "Reference Back Talk: Testing, Testing; Virtual Reference UX," *Library Journal* 138, no. 10 (2013), http://reviews.libraryjournal.com/.

15. Lili Luo, "Text Reference Service: Delivery, Characteristics, and Best Practices," *Reference Services Review* 39, no. 3 (2011): 482–96.

16. Erin Dorris Cassidy, Angela Colmenares, and Michelle Martinez, "So Text Me—Maybe," *Reference and User Services Quarterly* 53, no. 4 (2014): 300–312.

17. Monica Anderson, "Technology Device Ownership 2015," report, Pew Research Center, 2015, http://www.pewinternet.org/.

18. Lili Luo, "Text a Librarian: A Look from the Patron Perspective," *Reference Services Review* 42, no. 1 (2014): 34–51.

19. Lili Luo and Emily Weak, "Texting 4 Answers: What Questions Do People Ask?" *Reference and Patron Services Quarterly* 51, no. 2 (2011): 133–42.

20. Cassidy, Colmenares, and Martinez, "So Text Me."

21. David Ward, Maira I. Liriano, Betty A. Gard, and Rebecca L. Johnson, "Guidelines for Behavioral Performance of Reference and Information Service Providers," *Reference and Patron Services Quarterly* 44, no. 1 (2004): 14–17.

22. Maloney and Kemp, "Changes in Reference."

23. Duncan and Gerrard, "All Together Now!"

24. Kimberly K. Vardeman and Ian Barba, "Reference in 160 Characters or Less: The Role of Text Messaging in Virtual Reference Services," *Internet Reference Services Quarterly* 19, nos. 3–4 (2014): 163–79.

25. "About," Twitter, accessed May 16, 2016, https://about.twitter.com/company.

26. Valerie Forrestal, "Making Twitter Work: A Guide for the Uninitiated, the Skeptical, and the Pragmatic," *Reference Librarian* 52, nos. 1–2 (2010): 146–51.

27. Darcy Del Bosque, Sam A. Leif, and Susie Skarl, "Libraries Atwitter: Trends in Academic Library Tweeting," *Reference Services Review* 40, no. 2 (2012): 199–213.

28. Courtney L. Young, "Crowdsourcing the Virtual Reference Interview with Twitter," *Reference Librarian* 55, no. 2 (2014): 172–74.

29. Forrestal, "Making Twitter Work."

30. Scott Stone, "Breaking the Ice: Facebook Friending and Reference Interactions," *Reference and User Services Quarterly* 54, no. 1 (2014): 44–49.

31. Hofschire and Wanucha, "Public Library Websites."

32. Paula Barnett-Ellis and Charlcie Pettway Vann, "The Library Right There in My Hand: Determining Patron Needs for Mobile Services at a Medium-Sized Regional University," *Southeastern Librarian* 62, no. 2 (2014): 10–15.

33. William T. Caniano and Amy Catalano, "Academic Libraries and Mobile Devices: Patron and Reader Preferences," *Reference Librarian* 55, no. 4 (2014): 298–317.

34. Fred D. Barnhart and Jeannette E. Pierce, "Becoming Mobile: Reference in the Ubiquitous Library," *Journal of Library Administration* 52, nos. 6–7 (2012): 567.

Chapter Four

Choosing Newer and Better Staffing Models for Ways of Utilizing Staff

As the information needs of library patrons change, librarians are rethinking their reference staffing needs and models. More traditional models need to change, which can mean introducing a completely new model or altering an existing one. As the first three chapters discuss, library patrons have heightened expectations for convenient and personalized service, which has translated to an increased demand for models such as roving, consultation services, and virtual reference. Based on these expectations, there is more work for librarians to accomplish with either the same amount of staff or with even less staff. Therefore, a key challenge for librarians in moving forward with reference-service model development is maintaining commitment to excellent service while also developing alternative ways of providing that service.

One of these alternative ways is to leverage points of service across varying employee roles. For example, studies have shown that many reference questions do not need the skills of a professional librarian but instead can be answered by a well-trained paraprofessional. In addition, as the number of reference transactions has dropped in recent decades, librarians see even less reference transactions that require their knowledge and skills. Julie Banks and Carl Pracht provided a quantitative description of this trend in their survey of reference desk staffing trends in academic libraries. Specifically, they found that 86 percent of the libraries surveyed still had a reference desk. As previous chapters discuss, use of the reference desk, as traditionally conceived, has been shifting, and librarians need to embrace the changing ways in which the reference desk is used. One of the ways that libraries have been changing reference desk usage has been to staff the desk with paraprofessionals. Banks and Pracht found that 62 percent of academic libraries surveyed said that they used nonprofessionals at the reference desk and, further, that they used them "anytime"—not just evenings and weekends. The coverage by nonprofessionals was as high as 75 percent of the time, and only 64 percent of the respondents indicated that there was a librarian in the building at any given moment to answer more difficult questions. The respondents stated that they were not always comfortable with this arrangement, but it was unavoidable due to financial pressures along with other changes within the academic library environment. Many reasons were given by respondents for why nonprofessionals were used, such as needing coverage on evenings, weekends, and during meetings; being cost effective; and freeing up the librarians for other work such as instruction and virtual reference.[1]

In addition to changes in staffing, reference services have also experienced changes in regard to the types of reference questions asked. Specifically, libraries are experiencing a shift toward ready reference questions in lieu of more in-depth ones. For example, Bradley Bishop and Jennifer Bartlett at the University of Kentucky found that only 16 percent of the questions asked were subject based.[2] In another study, Scott Carlson at Temple University found that among over 4,400 reference questions asked in one month, only 5 percent involved extensive interaction and research, while 41 percent were directional.[3] In a third study, Susan Ryan at Stetson University found that of the total reference transactions in the period studied, 64 percent were directional or technology related, and 11 percent were research oriented.[4]

Based on this distribution of question types, how can libraries make the best use of their librarians? Specifically, how can libraries provide a reference experience to patrons when they do not appear to be asking questions eliciting this experience? Perhaps it may be that the act of responding to ready reference questions does not constitute a reference experience, and therefore it is important to reconceptualize what a reference experience implies. Given this thought, we, as librarians, should ask ourselves what constitutes a reference experience and how we can organize our staffing to provide that experience to our patrons. To answer this question, this chapter explores new staffing models that ensure good service for patrons while making maximum use of staff and providing a more cost-effective service. As librarians have seen the change in the kinds of reference questions asked and learned through surveys and that many of them can be answered by a paraprofessional or student, they have often decided to modify their staffing to a model that still provides good service but allows for better use of staff. This chapter provides an overview of these resultant staffing models.

STAFFING REFERENCE SERVICES WITHIN THE LIBRARY

Librarians can make many choices of how to provide good reference services and a good reference experience. One choice regards which type of employee to staff at each service point based on the dominant types of questions being asked. To this end, the Bishop and Bartlett study evaluated questions asked at the library's many service points based on quantity, quality, and question type. The authors also incorporated geographic data to find out where patrons were asking certain question types, namely, location-based and subject-based questions. Data was collected over a three-year period with findings indicating that, overall, the University of Kentucky library experienced a greater amount of location-based questions (84 percent) as compared to subject-based questions (16 percent). The authors also determined that both location- and subject-based questions were most often asked face-to-face. The majority of subject-based questions (37 percent) were asked at the Young Library reference desk, followed by at the Young Library periodicals and law library desks (15 percent each). By examining where the most subject-based questions were asked and the quantity of questions at each service point, Bishop and Bartlett derived key implications for library management to staff service points more effectively and strategically. Bishop and Bartlett also suggested that the findings could inform the design of mobile applications to fill gaps in service that may be created by restaffing various service points.[5]

At the Prior Health Sciences Library at Ohio State University, a slightly different model was developed. Due to decreasing demands for in-depth reference services, the library recognized that many questions could be answered by paraprofessionals. However, individuals still requiring assistance with in-depth reference questions had to return during reference desk hours, no formal referral system existed, and staffing the reference desk was problematic. To address these issues, the library reorganized its service in the following ways. First, staff members performed a gap analysis to identify gaps in their existing model and identified strategies to fill the gaps and an expected time frame to implement each strategy. These identified gaps and strategies informed the resultant proactive model. An assistance, service, and knowledge (ASK) desk was set up to answer routine questions and was staffed by paraprofessionals at all hours that the library was open. These paraprofessionals received extensive training. When the question required more in-depth assistance, the patron could be referred to a librarian. The referrals were all done by appointment. The interesting result of this new model was that the number of reference consultations lasting thirty minutes or more actually increased, which suggests an existing patron demand for reference services previously unmet by the older staffing model. Thus the library was able to both expand its liaison service and detract the number of hours that librarians spent providing reference services, while simultaneously meeting previously unaddressed patron needs. [6]

A similar staffing change occurred at Dickinson College. Theresa Arndt documented the quality and quantity of questions asked at the reference desk, as well as student perceptions of the reference desk, finding that that the rate of questions asked was one per hour with no definite peak times. A significant portion of questions asked (32 percent) were directional or reference questions that could be answered in five minutes or less. Additionally, students indicated confusion over how they should use the reference desk. For these reasons, coupled with the increased demand on librarians' time to teach information-literacy classes, the library decided to eliminate the physical reference desk in favor of an on-call/consultation model. To address concerns that the physical removal of the reference desk would denote to patrons that reference services were no longer available, the librarians left the desk in place but with a sign that directed patrons to the circulation desk for the first half of the semester following the elimination of the reference desk model. Since there were no complaints over this time period, the reference desk was eventually eliminated. The library's access services staff took over answering basic reference and directional questions, and referring more in-depth questions to the librarians after receiving training from the associate directors responsible for reference and instruction. In this model, librarians are always

Figure 4.1. A consultation with a patron.

available on call to work with patrons, including an on-call librarian who is responsible for staying near his or her office during a shift but able to do his or her own work when not assisting a student.

Crucial to this library's plan was the development of a reference marketing team, which advertised the new reference services in many places including ads in the campus newspapers, table tents in the library, posters in the library and elsewhere on campus, and a prominent sign for the Ask a Librarian service on the library's home page. In addition, the Ask a Librarian service developed a page for each subject specialist with information about their areas of specialization. The librarians thought that when they had a reference desk, the students did not understand what the librarians did. In their advertising, they explained how they could help patrons using Association of College and Research Libraries (ACRL) information-literacy competencies as a guiding framework.[7] These competencies included assistance with finding information, choosing the most relevant databases, improving research strategies, critically evaluating information, and citing sources properly. Librarians also marketed the service when providing information-literacy instruction to classes by mentioning the availability of reference services and asking faculty to include contact information for liaison libraries on class syllabi.[8] As in the case of the Prior Health Sciences Library, the result of these efforts was an increase in consultation appointments.[9] Perhaps one

Figure 4.2.   Librarian assisting a user but not at a reference desk.

could say that this increase was due to patrons being able to better understand what the librarians could do for them.

Based on findings from the studies discussed, as well as other studies examining the quality and quantity of questions asked, the reference desk is a place where many directional and ready reference questions are asked and answered. Many patrons are thus asking simple questions and wanting quick replies. Due to the nature of these questions, some libraries staff the reference desk with nonprofessionals and have librarians available on call to handle more complex questions. This staffing decision still leaves someone at an information desk so that patrons with questions will not have to guess where to go. Even though many questions asked at the reference desk may be quite simple, it is good customer service to have staff available. Sometimes the simple question does turn into a more complex one. This kind of model allows for maximum service but frees the librarian to work on other projects.

Best practices for an on-call/consultation model are as follows:

1. Be sure that nonprofessionals are well trained and that the training is updated frequently.
2. Be sure that training includes information about customer service, the library's resources and services, basic research skills, and the basic reference interview.
3. Be sure that clear guidelines have been established for when questions should be referred.
4. Try to have the on-call librarian at a reasonable distance from the reference/information desk so that the patron does not have to wait too long.
5. Have good publicity that lets patrons know that a librarian is always available to assist them and what the librarian can do for them.

Other libraries staff the information desk with a mix of staff, including some librarians and some nonlibrarians. In this model nonlibrarians are available to answer routine requests for information, but they share the information desk with librarians who can take over when needed or just serve as a second person at the desk to assist during busy times.

Best practices for this model, where there is a mix of librarians and nonprofessionals on the reference desk, are as follows:

1. Be sure that it is clear how this model works so that the staff knows what is expected of them.
2. Staff the reference desk at slow times with nonprofessionals, and add librarians at busy times.

3. Train the nonprofessionals well so they can field ready reference and directional questions and understand when to refer the patron to a librarian.

Some libraries have merged the reference desk and circulation desk into one service desk with a mix of reference and circulation staff responding to the questions. For example, at the Athens-Clarke County Library (Georgia) they combined service desks into a "concierge" desk staffed by a circulation clerk and a reference librarian, with other services nearby on the first floor. On the second floor a service desk is staffed by a reference librarian and an information technology (IT) librarian. The library developed this model to provide more personalized service by staffing the reference desks with individuals with various expertise.[10] In another case the Grand Valley State University Library moved from having a reference desk and circulation desk to a single point-of-service model. Before this merge took place, the librarians experimented to see how the various staffing models affected the number and type of questions asked. They documented the number of questions asked when a librarian staffed the reference desk versus when no librarian was at the desk but on call. They used various models in the test period with periods of reference staffing and periods of on-call staffing, and saw no change in the number of reference questions asked. As a result, they moved to the single service model. Based on the findings that there appeared to be no unmet needs for librarians staffing the reference desk, librarians continue to answer high-level questions but no longer have to answer ready reference and directional ones.[11]

Best practices for this model are as follows:

1. Train the nonprofessionals well so they can field ready reference and directional questions and understand when to refer the patron to a librarian.
2. Have librarians easily available so the patron does not have to wait.
3. Have clear guidelines for the on-call librarians so they have a schedule and someone is always available to assist the patron.
4. Make it clear through appropriate publicity that librarians are always available, and outline what they do for patrons.

The shift to models that staff paraprofessionals at specific points-of-reference service is also reflected in large-scale surveys of academic libraries. For example, Dennis Miles surveyed academic librarians and found that 83 percent of the libraries had at least one nonprofessional providing reference services. The importance of the reference desk was reflected by his finding that 66 percent provided reference services from a separate reference desk. At the reference desk, 49 percent of the staff was comprised of some librarians and some nonprofessionals, and 41 percent of reference desks were staffed at all times by a librarian. Roving reference was provided by 47 percent of the libraries, and in addition to the reference desk service, consultation services, which this chapter discusses, were offered by over 87 percent of libraries. For those libraries providing reference services outside the library, telephone and e-mail were the most popular (92 percent). When asked about staffing the reference desk in the future, 45 percent of the librarians still wanted to staff it with librarians all the time. This latter statistic to some degree may reflect a reticence of librarians to abandon the reference desk as a symbol of their traditional expert authority and points-of-service provision. [12]

Table 4.1.

Use of physical reference desk	• 86% of academic libraries surveyed still have a physical reference desk (Banks and Pracht 2008).
	• 66% of academic libraries surveyed still have a physical reference desk (Miles 2013).
	• Athens-Clarke County combined the reference and circulation desks into a concierge desk (Ames 2013).
Changes in staffing	• 62% of academic libraries surveyed staff the reference desk with nonprofessionals and use them "anytime" (Banks and Pracht 2008).
	• 64% of academic librarians surveyed are available anytime to answer research questions (Banks and Pracht 2008).
	• 83% of academic libraries surveyed staff reference desks with nonprofessionals (Miles 2013).
	• At the University of Kansas Library, librarians are on call, but nonprofessionals staff the reference desk (Devlin and Stratton 2013).
Changes in reference question types	• At Temple University, 41% of reference questions asked are directional, and 5% require extensive interaction (Carlson 2007).
	• At Stetson University, 64% of reference questions are directional or technology related, and 11% are research oriented (Ryan 2008).
	• At University of Kentucky, 16% of reference questions asked are subject based (Bishop and Bartlett 2013).
	• At Dickinson College, 32% of questions asked were directional or reference and could be answered in five minutes or less (Arndt 2010).
	• At the University of Arizona Library, 95% of questions can be answered by paraprofessionals (Bracke et al. 2007).
Services at point of need	• At the University of Kansas paraprofessionals provide staffing at specific desk locations with professionals at others (Devlin and Stratton 2013).
	• 47% of academic libraries surveyed offered roving reference (Miles 2013).
	• The Public Library of Cincinnati, Douglas Library, and the Johnson County Library all offer virtual call centers (Brehm-Heeger et al. 2013).
Specialized services	• The Prior Health Sciences Library at Ohio State University offers librarian consultation services (Schulte 2011).
	• At Dickinson College the librarian is on call (Arndt 2010).
	• Athens-Clarke County provides more specialized services by personalizing questions each reference desk addresses (Ames 2013).
	• 87% of academic libraries surveyed have librarian consultation services (Miles 2013).

- Texas Tech University and the University of San Diego offer personal librarians (Henry, Vardeman, and Syma 2012; Adkins 2015).

Evaluation and assessment of reference services

- University of Kentucky assessed who asked reference questions by geographic location (Bishop and Bartlett, 2013).
- At Prior Health Sciences Library, Ohio State University, the library performed a gap analysis to determine the best ways to provide needed services (Schulte 2011).
- Grand Valley State University analyzed the types of reference questions asked based on time and other contextual factors (Garrison 2011).
- The University of Arizona Library performed an action-gap analysis to decide how best to provide reference services (Bracke et al. 2007).
- The University of San Diego performed evaluation to determine the needs of students and how library can best meet these needs (Adkins 2015).

Marketing of services

- Dickinson College used signage to direct patrons to ask reference questions. The patrons' awareness of the services led to an increase in scheduled consultations (Arndt 2010).
- Texas Tech University saw 120% increase in use of personal librarian service offered by the library after marketing efforts (Henry, Vardeman, and Syma 2012).
- The University of San Diego marketed rollout of personal librarian services with campus-wide events (Adkins 2015).

RESEARCH CONSULTATIONS

As noted by findings of the studies discussed, many academic libraries perceive and experience viability within the interaction between librarians and patrons when implementing a consulting model. This research consultation model can work in different ways. It may be that the librarian is on call and the person at the information or reference desk makes the referral. In this case, staff must be trained well enough so they do not turn away a patron when they should have referred that patron to a librarian. Further, many libraries advertise the research consultation service to make patrons aware that they can go directly to a librarian for assistance. Used to address more extensive research questions, the research consultation gives the patron a chance to have a more in-depth conversation with a librarian, explore more aspects of his or her subject, and leave with information and resources. Although librarians have not always offered this service, it is an important one that both expands the role of the librarian using his or her skills and expertise, and personalizes the service for the patron. Patrons can learn through this experience the value of a librarian and the knowledge he or she brings to bear on a reference question. Expanding reference services beyond the traditional desk makes patrons understand that the librarian is capable of more than just answering ready reference questions. Using the Reference and User Services Association's (RUSA) definition of a reference transaction as "information consultations in which library staff recommend, interpret, evaluate, and/or use information resources to help others to meet particular information needs,"[13] it becomes apparent that the consultation model represents an extension, rather than a removal or gradual weaning, of reference services. In many libraries such an extension represents a necessary shift in how patrons use reference services.

CASE STUDIES

Several recent case studies exemplify how different academic and public libraries have responded to the shifting needs and requirements for reference services. The University of Arizona Library had already reorganized its staff in the 1990s. During the original reorganization, the librarians moved from traditional functions such as reference and cataloging to being part of a team that served a particular customer group, such as the Science-Engineering Team or the Undergraduate Services Team, and were responsible for many activities including collection management and instruction. In 2003, they were faced with university-wide budget cuts that resulted in the loss of staff positions and thus the extent to which resources from the initial reorganization could be employed. To address the consequences of these cuts, the library made changes in the way they provided service based on several studies. The first study used question logs as its primary mode of data collection. Library staff logged every reference question they received by location for three two-week periods. Each question was analyzed by type and the level of employee needed to answer it, with findings indicating that the majority of questions (95 percent) could be addressed by trained paraprofessionals. Next, to capture how patrons perceived the quality of services provided, the librarians implemented a customer-driven action process survey technique, where respondents could indicate the five most important services the library offered, which five services it did best, and the five services most in need of improvement. These services ranged from "Help identifying articles and/or books for your research topic" to "Making sure we understand your question."[14] These resultant responses were put into charts that graphically displayed the results along the following criteria: which services were most important, net performance (services the organization did best minus services in need of improvement), and an action-gap analysis based on all three survey services. A final mode of data collection estimated the costs of specific services, with the salaries of specialist librarians constituting the largest cost. Based on this latter finding, coupled with findings from question log data that demonstrated a decreasing need for subject specialists in addressing more in-depth reference questions, the library staff decided to combine the reference and circulation desks in science-engineering and in fine arts. Based on the higher volume of reference requests experienced at the information commons, the library staff decided to staff it with a small group of full-time employees. The library also upgraded the referral procedure to provide real-time support by having staff contact the subject specialist directly, who would then suggest how the staff should proceed. To further eliminate the amount of time spent by, and thus the cost of, librarians on the reference desk, the library staff made a final change by offering chat reference services from the information commons help desk and training more staff members so they could extend the chat service coverage. All these changes provided additional time for the librarians to participate in other important projects and provided necessary cost savings for the library.[15]

Another case study involves the University of Kansas Libraries, who described their evolving reference staffing as follows: in 2002, to better use library staff time, the library merged the separate reference units in two libraries into one unit. In 2004, a "peer and tier" model was developed where students and paraprofessionals staffed the desks and the librarians were on call.[16] Paraprofessionals from other library departments were asked to volunteer to work on the desk, and those that volunteered were appropriately trained. More reorganization took place in 2005 with the dissolution of the merged reference department, but the peer-and-tier model retained. The staff volunteers were also retained, and IT staff members were added at the service desk. However, a 2006 LibQUAL survey indicated that the model was not working, with students expressing dissatisfaction with the reference services provided. To address these survey results, the library, since 2007, has again staffed the service desk with librarians, library staff from other units, and graduate student assistants. Similar to subject specialists, the staff members from other departments who also participate in these points of service are now called research specialists. The service desk remained in one unit, but in another unit a "learning studio" was developed, which was an information desk shared with staff from IT, reference, and Student Success.[17] Similar to the consequences from other studies reviewed, using paraprofessionals has freed up librarians for other professional activities, but as this case study denotes, paraprofessionals must be employed strategically at points of service that adequately address patron needs.[18]

The Arlington Heights Memorial Library (Illinois) represents a case study from a public library. All face-to-face information services (i.e., reception, advisory, reference, magazines, and newspapers) have been combined into one desk—information services. Staff members from the information services desk also rove to identify patrons who may need assistance. Requests for information made outside the library such as via phone, e-mail, chat, and so forth, are handled through a call center. The staff uses walkie-talkies to communicate with each other.[19]

PERSONAL LIBRARIANS

An offset of the concept of the librarian as a consultant has also been offered by academic libraries that have developed personal librarian programs. These programs are often more marketing based and focus on making librarians approachable to students with subject-oriented reference questions. A case study from Texas Tech University exemplifies how a personal library strategy can be implemented. The library began to promote the subject librarians as personal librarians. To promote this concept, the staff recorded videos of the librarians discussing their hobbies and work responsibilities, and providing their contact information at the end of the video. The videos were circulated using social media, including being posted on the libraries' YouTube channel, Facebook page, and on a web page created for each personal librarian. Based on the reception of these videos, the amount of student meetings grew 120 percent in two years. The personal librarians also adopted a type of roving reference to their service model by moving outside the library with a mobile unit to answer questions on campus, further instilling the notion of their overall approachability.[20]

At the University of San Diego, the library contacted all the new students by letter, introducing a personal librarian program and telling the students

Figure 4.3. Librarian providing good customer service.

who their personal librarian would be. At the end of the first week of classes, a New Student Bash was held at the library with food, games, and fun tours of the library. During the year the personal librarians sent out e-mails promoting library events and workshops. The librarians continually emphasized ways that students could get in touch with the library, such as virtual reference services, social media, and self-guided tours. The library reported that as a result of the personal librarian program, it has been afforded additional opportunities to interact with both students and the faculty to determine which elements of reference services are perceived by students to be most useful. Based on these findings, the library now has "a three-pronged service model: information-literacy instruction in the classroom or library as arranged between discipline faculty and liaison librarians, point-of-need instruction and assistance at the reference desk, and contact between students and librarians outside of the library, outside the classroom."[21]

VIRTUAL REFERENCE SERVICES

Many reference questions are not posed by patrons at the physical library. Rather the questions come by e-mail, chat, and text messaging. Staffing of virtual reference services poses a number of issues such as needing someone to coordinate scheduling and providing resources to support the librarians assigned to this service. Staff need to be aware of library policies about the patrons the library will serve, how questions will be handled including the response time expected, and if there are any limitations of types of questions that will be answered. The library may want to develop triage models that can refer questions to specialists if necessary and determine available hours of operation. There is also the possibility of using crowdsourcing to answer questions.[22] Libraries must also determine how to staff e-mail, chat, SMS (Short Message Service), text messaging, and other virtual services. Making this determination requires careful scheduling for the services to run smoothly. Staffing virtual reference services from the reference desk may be difficult if the reference desk is busy. On the other hand, if the librarians are on call for the reference desk, they can be available for chat, SMS, and text-messaging requests for service. In other libraries, a separate staffing schedule has been developed to make the staff readily available to those requesting service from chat, SMS, text messaging, and other services. Those who are assigned with providing virtual reference services can provide the service from their desks while doing other work since the number of requests may vary by day of the week and hour of the day.

Many public libraries have set up a call center to respond to questions received using communication modalities other than face-to-face. For example, the Public Library of Cincinnati and Hamilton County (PLCHC) has established a Virtual Information Center (VIC). This separate service "focuses on: assisting customers with the library's e-book and downloadable collection; creating content for the library's website; answering circulation and ready reference questions; and responding to patron questions submitted via e-mail, text and the patron comments section of the website."[23] Other libraries with call centers include Douglas County Libraries (Colorado) and Johnson County Library (Kansas).[24] Based on the successes and failures of these call centers, some best practices for libraries planning to set up a call center include the following:

1. Add new technologies as they become available and are used by the library's community.
2. Provide information to patrons as to how the service works.
3. Monitor data to make the best use of the service.
4. Develop partnerships with other local organizations who can answer patron questions.
5. Have staff assist in the planning and implementation of the service.
6. Train staff and update the training often.

STAFFING NEW MODELS FOR REFERENCE SERVICES

Staffing of new models for reference services requires a great deal of planning. There are many considerations. The number of staff available is paramount as well as the needs of the patron body. What works well in one situation may not in another. The way the transition is made can also be important for both the staff and patrons. Surveys, focus groups, and so forth, can help the library understand how to move forward. In her article on reference services without the desk, Arndt posed the following questions that can help librarians to think about what kind of staffing is best for their library:

1. What is the library's philosophy of reference services? What level of reference questions should a librarian be answering?
2. If there is a reference desk, what is the level of traffic? Is the staffing appropriate for the level of traffic?
3. What is the patrons' perception of reference services, do they understand the difference between librarians and other staff members, and do they understand what services are available?
4. Has the library calculated the cost of reference services?
5. What other work do the librarians have, and does other work not get done because the librarians are staffing the reference desk?
6. How can the local characteristics of patrons be matched with various reference models?[25]

These questions begin to get at the heart of the reference desk and staffing issues. There is a great deal of documentation indicating that not staffing the reference desk with librarians or not having a reference desk does not eliminate the need for librarians. Studies cited earlier in this chapter indicate that patrons move quickly to consultation services, and the number of patrons asking for assistance does not diminish and sometimes actually increases.

CONCLUSION

The reference model that an individual library chooses must meet that library's needs. The subject of meeting patron reference needs should be studied at a local level, and perhaps more than one model should be tried before a final decision is made. Two things are quite clear from the studies being done: first, patrons do not always understand what services are available at a reference desk; and second, often a strong consultation service will have more patrons that ask in-depth reference questions. All communities and all patrons are not the same so libraries must judge what staffing patterns work best. Patrons are more flexible than librarians think, and a new staffing pattern with appropriate communication with the patrons can be successful. For the patrons the important thing is getting assistance in a timely manner.

NOTES

1. Julie Banks and Carl Pracht, "Reference Desk Staffing Trends: A Survey," *Reference and Patron Services Quarterly* 48, no. 1 (2008): 54–59.

2. Bradley Wade Bishop and Jennifer A. Bartlett, "Where Do We Go from Here? Informing Academic Library Staffing through Reference Transaction Analysis," *College and Research Libraries* 74, no. 5 (2013): 489–500.

3. Scott Carlson, "Are Reference Desks Dying Out? Librarians Struggle to Redefine—and in Some Cases Eliminate—the Venerable Institution," *Reference Librarian* 48, no. 2 (2007): 25–30.

4. Susan M. Ryan, "Reference Transactions Analysis: The Cost-Effectiveness of Staffing a Traditional Academic Reference Desk," *Journal of Academic Librarianship* 34, no. 5 (2008): 389–99.

5. Bishop and Bartlett, "Where Do We Go from Here?"

6. Stephanie J. Schulte, "Eliminating Traditional Reference Services in an Academic Health Sciences Library: A Case Study," *Journal of the Medical Library Association* 99, no. 4 (2011): 273–79.

7. "Information Literacy Competency Standards for Higher Education," Association of College and Research Libraries, accessed June 23, 2016, http://www.ala.org/.

8. Theresa S. Arndt, "Reference Service without the Desk," *Reference Services Review* 38, no. 1 (2010): 71–80.

9. Schulte, "Eliminating Traditional Reference."

10. Kathryn Ames, e-mail message to author, July 10, 2013.

11. Julie Garrison, "What Do We Do Now? A Case for Abandoning Yesterday and Making the Future," *Reference and User Services Quarterly (RUSQ)* 51, no. 1 (2011): 12–15.

12. Dennis B. Miles, "Shall We Get Rid of the Reference Desk?" *Reference and Patron Services Quarterly* 52, no. 4 (2013): 320–33.

13. "Definitions of Reference," Reference and User Services Association (RUSA), accessed June 23, 2016, http://www.ala.org/.

14. Marianne Stowell Bracke et al., "Finding Information in a New Landscape: Developing New Service and Staffing Models for Mediated Information Services," *College and Research Libraries* 68, no. 3 (2007): 263.

15. Ibid., 248–67.

16. Frances Devlin and John Stratton, "Evolving Models of Reference Staffing at the University of Kansas Libraries," *Research Library Issues*, no. 282 (2013): 21.

17. Ibid., 23.

18. Ibid., 21–26.

19. Nancy K. Phillips, "Reference Renovation," *ILA Reporter* 32, no. 2 (2014): 12–15.

20. Cynthia L. Henry, Kimberly K. Vardeman, and Carrye K. Syma, "Reaching Out: Connecting Students to Their Personal Librarian," *Reference Services Review* 40, no. 3 (2012): 396–407.

21. Martha Adkins, "Meet Your Personal Librarian," in *Reimagining Reference in the 21st Century*, ed. David A. Tyckoson and John G. Dove (West Lafayette, IN: Purdue University Press, 2015), 179.

22. Joe Murphy, "Management Models and Considerations for Virtual Reference," *Science and Technology* 29, nos. 1–2 (2010): 178.

23. Paula Brehm-Heeger et al., "Library Call Centers: Five Unique Examples," *Public Libraries* 52, no. 6 (2013): 33.

24. Ibid., 32–26.

25. Arndt, "Reference Service."

Chapter Five

Providing Outreach

Outreach services can be defined as moving out from the traditional reference services offered within the library. All libraries have many potential user groups beyond their four walls who simply do not frequent the library often or at all. They need and welcome library services but for many reasons do not take advantage of them. As below case studies illustrate, potential users may not be aware that the library is equipped to address information needs beyond basic reference questions, such as finding articles on a particular subject. Many approaches to library service, especially reference, are being tried to reach new audiences. This approach to reference looks different depending on the type of library and the community it serves. As a result, several outreach programs including embedded librarianship, community reference, and information literacy are explored in this chapter. Case studies and new approaches of reference outreach services are also described.

OUTREACH IN PUBLIC LIBRARIES

Public libraries have traditionally done a great deal of outreach because they were aware that many of their users did not come to the library. Outreach involved moving out into the communities, for instance, by attending community meetings to tell prospective patrons about the public library's collections and services. In some cases outreach placed a strong emphasis on reference and information services such as how to use databases; and in others, a more general emphasis on all aspects of library services.

Outreach services are often jointly achieved by partnerships between public libraries and local government and community groups. Sometimes a grant opportunity causes them to work together, such as a joint digitization project, and sometimes collaboration derives from a common area of interest, such as increasing attendance at relevant library workshops. These partnerships result in the two groups meeting and talking either in person or virtually. As a result of their partnership, not only do the groups understand each other much better in regard to how their organizations function and the contributions they can make, but also the librarian understands more about the information needs of the proposed user groups and can offer a new level of services.

More often than not these partnerships must be initiated by the library since most groups have no idea of the wealth of information resources that a librarian has available. Sometimes because these groups make the assumption that the level of reference work the library offers is fairly basic, they do not realize that the librarian has the tools to do much more. Maybe the users think the librarian can help them find the price of a used car or direct them to material to help write a resume. What they do not realize is that the librarian can also find information on how to negotiate a contract or how to write a business plan.

In light of these assumptions, among other factors, moving outside the four walls of the library has become an increasingly popular idea. Many people need library services, but not all of them actually visit a library. This lack of visitation happens for many reasons. People may have an information need but be too busy to visit the library and not realize that they can ask questions through a library chat service. In order to reach a new clientele, libraries must move outward and reach out to new audiences. This outreach is not limited to public libraries. In fact, any library, including academic and school libraries, can reach beyond its walls and introduce its services to community members. The key idea linking any outreach service is that the library, as it moves into the community, must think about mutually beneficial collaborations, partnerships, and entrepreneurial ventures. These new ways of reaching the library's users can change the way they see the library and what it has to offer.

COMMUNITY REFERENCE

While libraries have been performing elements of community reference for a while, envisioning these elements as an integrated service is very new. Early adopters of what is called "community reference" or "embedded librarianship" were the Douglas County Libraries in Castle Rock, Colorado. The director, Jamie LaRue, believed that "librarians have the power to change lives and build community—but to do this, we have to leave our desks, leave our buildings and show the community what a powerful tool we are."[1] The Douglas County Libraries project began when LaRue and others on the staff began to notice that while fewer questions were being asked at the physical reference desk, many community groups asked questions at community meetings that could be answered by library research. Librarians engaged in community reference by meeting and interviewing community leaders, elected officials, representatives from the schools, nonprofits, and religious groups to determine their information-related goals as well as what research could help them to make more informed decisions to achieve these goals. Some of the initial issues librarians worked on included "how to replace Parker's (one of the communities in Douglas County) sewer lines and whether it would be better to put in angled or parallel parking spots in town. . . . A reference librarian was assigned to research those issues, ultimately resulting in an entire economic development study."[2]

This initial project translated into a well-defined outreach plan that has embedded reference librarians in key community organizations. Librarians spend at least four hours a week in the community, such as at a local senior center or at meetings of community organizations, and work with a wide array of community and governmental groups. This work has made a big impact on the community by bringing the library to the attention of its leaders, who view the library as enacting civic engagement by researching community issues and providing library services to community groups as appropriate.

Examples of community reference projects include compiling research on the history of Colorado's medical marijuana law and local regulations on marijuana dispensaries to inform the community on how it might impose its

Figure 5.1.   Community is of great importance to libraries.

own regulations; collecting photos of local historical figures to create a walking tour of the downtown area; and investigating the proposed economic impact a college would have on the area. Working with community groups has enabled the library to strategically restructure traditional services to fulfill community needs. For instance, the library now visits the Women's Crisis and Family Outreach Center weekly to provide library cards, books, movies, and other items to families in the shelter. Librarians have also provided computer and resume-writing workshops. Another library in Douglas County helped develop a boot camp for area businesses, which included a library resource guide for entrepreneurs and small businesses. Rather than envision why these groups were not visiting the library, the Douglas County librarians instead saw the potential for offering their services outside of the library's physical confines and thus reaching out to a broader constituency.

Unlike traditional reference models, the Douglas County librarians seek out community groups with which to work. These groups could be key community groups, groups with a problem that the librarians found organically, or groups who requested a librarian. To get started, librarians attend community meetings to determine if each group they visit would be good for a mutually beneficial partnership. Their criteria for partnership include the following:

1. The group adds value to the community.
2. The library is essential to the group achieving its goals.
3. Participating in the group helps the library to be more visible and valuable to the community.

Decisions as to what groups to work with are made carefully. Staff members say that businesses and local government are usually good places to start. As relationships with community organizations develop over time, it becomes easier to identify other potential opportunities for engagement. Knowledge of these opportunities is codified by librarians in an internal community reference blog where they contribute information on their projects and what is happening in the community. The blog is exceedingly valuable because the librarians can identify overarching themes that describe more than one community or community group to give them ideas as to how to allocate their time. They report on local issues and include minutes from government and community meetings, and updates on current projects, as well as interviews with local leaders. By working this way, the librarians can not only sustain current partnerships but also identify emerging group issues, develop a relationship with the stated group, and cultivate an in-depth understanding of the project and work to be done. These goals are embodied by the librarians' mantra to "show up, pay attention and stay in touch." The librarians are also asked to build assessment into each project by asking those assisted if the library's contribution was valuable.[3]

In 2011 the Douglas County Libraries pushed themselves even further into the community by setting up a series of interviews with local community leaders to find out more about the issues that faced the county. Through recording interview observations on the blog, the librarians gained a deeper understanding of county residents and how they could address these needs. Library programming was then developed based on issues they uncovered. This process also served for librarians to make valuable contacts with local leaders. Based on the success of this initiative, another round of interviews is planned for a later date.[4]

The Deschutes Public Library in Oregon began a community library in-itiative after a survey indicated that many local residents did not use the library, although they thought they should. Based on this perceived need for library services by local residents who, for a multitude of reasons, might not visit the library's physical location, it became obvious to the library director that the library needed to get out into the five communities that they served. The library developed a plan for outreach to community groups and commit-tees. In achieving this plan, key committees and groups in the community that librarians should connect with were identified. The librarians were asked to spend 25 to 33 percent of their time in the community. The library worked closely with local businesses, meeting with them one by one to provide information about the library's resources including databases. The library also ran workshops on resume writing and job resources for a statewide network devoted to helping citizens find employment and at a community college. Moving out into the community enabled the librarians to identify new information needs that they could meet. The result was a large jump in library use (from 35 percent in 2007 to 60 percent in 2012) and reference transactions (from sixty-five thousand to one hundred thousand over the past four years) as well as continued work with community groups and organiza-tions.[5]

As the two outlined case studies suggest, there are several steps that can be taken to initiate community outreach. The community reference model includes the following components:

1. A community survey
2. An analysis of the needs of businesses, nonprofits, community com-mittees, and groups
3. A plan for moving forward that includes both the outreach efforts and how the library will be staffed when librarians are engaged in outreach projects
4. A preliminary list of possible projects

5. A way for outreach staff to communicate on a regular basis, such as the internal blog used in Douglas County
6. Guidelines for the outreach staff of what criteria they will use in identifying and developing a new project
7. A description of what success will look like
8. An evaluation plan
9. A description of how to judge when it is time to move on to other projects

Staffing for outreach efforts can follow several paths. In both of the case studies outlined, the libraries had all librarians providing outreach services. However, in the Jefferson County Library, Colorado, the library designates outreach or specialist librarians available to provide more in-depth services or to come to speak to individuals and groups. Areas of librarian expertise include employment and business support, school success (early literacy and homework help), family wellness, Spanish services, services to special populations, digital content creation, and digital literacy. Similar to the other case studies, the Jefferson County Library also developed information about the issues and priorities of their users based on surveys and interviews with community and business leaders. The emerging themes included literacy/education support, economic development support, and community development support. All this information is used in the development of collections and programs.[6]

Aside from using surveys or interviews to capture community needs, libraries can also present preidentified groups with a plan outlining how librarians' skill sets can align with a group's information needs. For example, in another community case study, two library staff members began by selecting local businesses to contact. They then visited each business and told them about library services, especially the library's expertise with the Internet and social media. They also discussed with each business what resources the library had that might be useful to them, finding that many needed help getting their message out on social media or other resources the library could provide.[7]

All of the case studies discussed suggest that while there are certain steps that can be taken to achieve community outreach, the way these steps are actualized vary based on resources within the library, such as staffing, as well as community-based needs. However, the decision to implement outreach services must first be made before considering such logistics.

OUTREACH AMONG TYPES OF LIBRARIES

An important role for both public and academic librarians is providing outreach to schools. There is no exact formula for how to work with them. Often the best person to start with is the school librarian, who can inform on what is being taught and resources the schools might need from the public library. Many public librarians plan to visit classes once a year to introduce the public library and sign students up for library cards. The summer reading program can be a good time to make this visit since traditionally students use the public library more in the summer. But once a strong relationship is formed between libraries and schools, there will be many opportunities for collaboration. For example, some public libraries and schools share their online catalog while others coordinate collection development. In other communities the public librarians present new resources for public school teachers. The more school and public libraries can work together, the better.

Outreach to schools is not limited to public libraries. Many academic libraries also work with school libraries. Academic libraries can also share resources with school libraries, especially LibGuides and presentations about using an academic library. Some academic libraries provide for visits by students so that they can get an idea of what an academic library is like. An article by Katelyn Angell and Eamon Tewell discusses collaboration among Sarah Lawrence College Library, the Yonkers Public Library, and the Yonkers High School to this effect. [8]

Public and school libraries can also combine resources. Matthew Lighthart and Creedence Spreder wrote about the Pungo-Blackwater Public Library and the Creeds Elementary School Library sharing space and resources in a Virginia Beach community that could not afford two libraries. The partnership has worked well for both libraries and has enabled the community to have one good library on a limited budget. [9]

Carrie Rogers-Whitehead, Lorelei Rutledge, and Jacob Reed detailed a collaboration between the University of Utah and Salt Lake County Libraries to create tutorials to help librarians understand available, accessible technologies and how to use them to provide better service to patrons. [10] Another public and academic library partnership on health information was among the St. Louis Public Library, the Beeker Medical Library at Washington University, and the National Cancer Institute–funded program at the Sherman Cancer Center at Washington University. This partnership administered hands-on training for the St. Louis Public Library staff on providing reliable health information, and installed four kiosks in library branches with health information and health-related programs on such subjects as prenatal care, oral health, eye health, complementary and alternative medicine, mental health, bullying, and cancer. As the partnership progressed, the programs turned to exercise, nutrition, and stress relief. [11]

READER'S ADVISORY

Reader's advisory has become a popular part of public library reference and now encompasses fiction, nonfiction, and media. Users want information on new books to read and books that fit their reading interests. However, many users are surprised to learn that the library will recommend books for leisure reading since they have not thought of using the reference librarian as a source for this sort of information.

The Wilkinson Public Library in Telluride, Colorado, wanted to show their users that there was more to reference than just answering questions. To introduce a reader's advisory service to users, the library created BookMatch, a monthly program/service held in the main lobby where librarians sit at a table with information on new books and a computer. The program/service is extremely flexible. Librarians can just talk to users and suggest books to read, or the user can fill out a form to get the conversation started. The form has three items to answer: "Tell us about a book you read recently and enjoyed. Tell us a little about your current interest. Is there a particular author you particularly dislike? Who? Why?"[12]

Although it always begins with a resource recommendation, reader's advisory services are broad and can lead to other kinds of information services once the user is comfortable contacting the librarian for assistance.

OUTREACH IN COLLEGE AND UNIVERSITY LIBRARIES

Outreach in academic libraries has been defined as collaborating with public libraries and school libraries, working with community organizations and public institutions as well as with groups on campus, and reaching out beyond the library to nontraditional user groups. It can be as broad or narrow as the library wants to make it. As the many articles on outreach in academic libraries indicate, outreach does not necessarily cost a great deal of money. It is more a matter of taking advantage of opportunities to work with other academic units and organizations on campus and the community where the college or university is located. By working with others the library can take advantage of opportunities to reach more students and faculty on campus and beyond, and share the costs of the project. As experience has shown, there are possibilities for collaboration with almost any academic unit, department, or organization. Libraries simply need to be aware of what resources they can bring to the table and think flexibly about how to participate in a particular event.[13]

The library at the Indiana University–Purdue, Fort Wayne (IPFW), campus developed a spreadsheet to document their collaboration and outreach activities called the Collaboration Index. This index identified ways that the library was reaching out to the community and campus. Community outreach included an American Library Association (ALA)–National Endowment for the Humanities (NEH) grant for the Muslim Journeys project, which involved both the campus and the community, digitization projects that involved community partners, joint campus/community events, and library staff service to community organizations. Campus outreach included programs to support undergraduate and graduate student outreach such as hosting a poster symposium in the library's learning commons. The poster symposium demonstrated the potential for how broad outreach efforts could potentially get. Librarians did not just host the symposium but also participated in the organizing committee for the symposium and offered workshops on developing poster content, using technology to create the posters, and assistance in researching the content for the poster. Through library facilitation, the posters were then included in OPUS, the university's scholarly repository. The library also works on other campus design projects, presentations, and posters. The library is working to develop ongoing relationships with other campus units and be part of new faculty orientations. The work of the IPFW library shows the many directions collaboration and outreach can take.[14]

Many librarians have found it effective to have a regular station on campus in some place other than the library. This station could be in a student center, busy classroom building, or dormitory. Librarians report that multipurpose locations work best because students are coming to these locations for a wide variety of purposes. Librarians implementing this service say that while it can lead to an increased amount of reference questions, it also makes the students more aware of the library and perhaps allows them to feel more comfortable when visiting the library in knowing they will find a familiar face when they do. By moving closer to the users, the library develops an active relationship with them.

Steven Bell said in his often-quoted article "Who Needs a Reference Desk?" that information-literacy instruction is a form of "pre-emptive reference."[15] Information literacy is also a form of library outreach. Information literacy initiatives often involve librarians visiting classes and making presentations about the library. Information literacy can have many formats depending on what the librarian wants to accomplish and the time frame available. Although many still prefer a short presentation, interactive presentations often are better since they are more likely to engage the class in the subject. It has also been determined that the best time for librarians to give a presentation is when the students are about to begin a project that involves the library since they are at the point of need and more focused on finding information for a specific project. Otherwise they may forget what they have learned by the time they are assigned the project. Information literacy not only provides resources to students but also introduces the students to the library and the librarian. This introduction means that as the students need further assistance, they know that they can go to the librarian who did the presentation. Once again, the student is not walking into the library without any contact information, and this helps to ease his or her anxiety about entering into an unknown situation.

A great part of the outreach of academic librarians revolves around their role as liaison to a department. As department liaisons, librarians make regular visits to a particular department to answer questions and make the faculty and graduate students aware of library services and new resources. Often called "embedded librarianship," "it emphasizes the importance of forming a strong working relationship between the librarian and a group or team of people who need the librarian's information expertise" (see also the "Outreach in Public Libraries" section of this chapter).[16] One of the strategies for forming this relationship is having librarians maintain a schedule of office hours so that faculty and students know when they will be there. Jerremie Clyde and Jennifer Lee reported that the benefits of embedded librarianship include

> increased visibility of the librarian within the department leading to collaborative course design, involvement by the librarian in departmental meetings and committees, increased awareness on the part of the librarian about faculty service and collection needs, and a more casual working relationship with faculty and students making them more willing to ask the librarian for research assistance.[17]

Some librarians who have had challenges in working successfully with a department have developed successful approaches to do so over time. The University of Houston reported on an environmental scan of its outreach activities to determine some of the more effective approaches. Findings indicated that personalized contact received the best response and that the most effective ways to contact the faculty were person to person, e-mail, and phone. Specific messages such as information for a particular class received more attention. But a general message to faculty combined with personal follow-up was also effective. For those librarians having trouble building a relationship with a department, it was suggested that they find advocates who could talk about the role of the library and help to get more people in the department interested in what they had to offer. The Houston study also indicated that it usually takes at least three years for a library liaison to be trusted, respected, and thus accepted in a department as part of its research team. Just like the next study discussed, the University of Houston found that one approach did not fit all situations and librarians had to be creative and find what worked for them.[18]

The University of Calgary Library reported on a six-year experiment with embedded librarianship. Specifically, this form of embedded librarianship

Figure 5.2. Librarian communicating with a user by phone.

assigned the librarians as liaisons to specific departments where they were allowed to set up their own relationship to those departments. As an example, some liaison librarians began to attend departmental meetings and engage in collaborative course design with faculty. What this report found is that although the relationship may start in the physical space, such as a faculty member meeting with a librarian during the latter's office hours, the greatest success comes "when the librarians become part of the patrons' mental workspace or community."[19] And although there may be some general guidelines for how to work as a liaison, the librarian must have the freedom to design the service to meet the needs of his or her patrons. So all liaison services will not look the same, even within the same university, as different departments will have varying needs.

In regard to the on-site time requirements to work as a liaison librarian, spending enough time on-site is important. This time might be as little as two hours or as much as six hours or more a week. In addition to just being available on-site, liaison libraries also often meet one to one with faculty members to discuss issues such as information-literacy presentations, and also meet one to one and in small groups with students to perform activities such as answering questions about research needs. The University of Calgary study noted that as a result of adopting these initiatives, liaison librarians were invited to attend faculty meetings or to join a faculty committee. They were also often invited to teach a course. Through engaging in these activities, they then became part of the departmental faculty and were invited to departmental activities. All of these responses combined signified that liaison librarians came to know more about the work of the faculty and thus were better at providing the kind of services and support needed. [20]

Libraries can also provide outreach for more traditional reference services. The University of New Mexico began to see their amount of reference desk transactions decreasing so they decided to redefine the role of reference in the library by engaging more with their community. Specifically, they envisioned reference as shifting from answering questions at a desk to providing learning, researching, and discovery spaces. To address this shift, they developed what they called "reverse reference": "taking reference librarians off the desk and allowing them to engage with their communities fosters trusted relationships, valuable partners and opens up collaboration opportunities."[21] The library developed the Ambassador program, which reorganized the subject specialists into subject clusters to work more closely with the faculty and students, integrating librarians into the research process. The library also established the VDS (Virtual Service Desk) as an easy way for the patrons to contact the library for assistance by creating a one-stop shopping for reference services with one phone number, one e-mail account, and one chat account. This consolidation of accounts resulted in a 56 percent increase in the use of the VDS and an increase in referrals to subject experts.

Based on some of the lessons learned from the aforementioned case studies in this section, below are some guidelines for engaging in liaison work:

1. Meet with the members of the academic department or other academic unit face-to-face and get to know the people.
2. Request to speak briefly at a faculty meeting.
3. Set up regular times to be in the department based on what seems to be appropriate.
4. Be friendly and start hallway conversations.
5. Network and identify influential department contacts.
6. Keep in touch with the faculty in the department. Send out e-mails on a regular basis promoting new library services and resources.
7. Respond to individual requests for assistance.
8. Provide personal orientations and tours.
9. Attend departmental events such as student capstones.
10. Become familiar with individual faculty research.
11. Refer faculty to specialists in the library on such issues as copyright, open access, and digital management.
12. Write congratulatory notes to faculty regarding research, publications, grants, and awards.
13. Welcome and provide orientation for new faculty.

14. Develop strong subject expertise, and provide workshops on resources in the subject area.
15. Get to know student groups, go to their meetings, and make presentations. [22]

BUSINESS AND ENTREPRENEURIAL OUTREACH

Many public and academic libraries have developed business centers or centers that encourage entrepreneurial activities. These centers are located in the library but are usually in conjunction with other local organizations such as the Small Business Development Center, SCORE, and chamber of commerce. This kind of project is one that strengthens connections to the community and provides meaningful reference service.

Academic libraries are not solely constrained to providing services for students and faculty. Although all library resources are not available to nonuniversity people, they are available if the person comes to the library. For instance, the University of Nevada at Las Vegas Library developed an outreach program to the surrounding business community. The director took the lead in this endeavor by reaching out to business people within the community and presenting on how libraries can assist professionals with business research, as well as other kinds of research and services, such as how to prepare a resume. She eventually became an active member of the Rotary Club. The director introduced the business librarian to various groups, and the business librarian provided workshops and presentations, as well as individual consultations and resource guides. The librarians also gave presentations on different aspects of business, such as how to use business research to develop business plans and find information to support a business start-up. These presentations used scenarios that depicted realistic examples of how someone can go from an idea to a business plan using library resources. [23]

Other academic and public libraries have developed similar programs. The business and business start-up communities are good for library outreach by both public and academic libraries. In a public library context, the Middle Country (New York) Public Library set up the Miller Business Resource Center. This center offers a wide range of resources and services for business people and entrepreneurs. In terms of resources, the center has reference and circulating collections of books, periodicals, and media, as well as many databases and computers with design programs installed, and a 3-D printer. The library also works closely with the Stony Brook (a local university) Small Business Development Center and the local chamber of commerce to develop programming and services appropriate for this user community. One example of such programming is offering business programs on a regular basis to encourage networking. [24] Another public library endeavor is at the

Business and Career Library, which is a stand-alone branch of the Brooklyn Public Library (New York). In addition to providing reference services, the Business and Career Library offers classes, counseling, and workshops on business-related topics. The library works with SCORE and Workforce1. They have also formed a Success Council with members of economic development groups, banks, and local businesses. This council provides suggestions for programs, speakers, new funding, and new initiatives. [25]

At Texas A&M one of the business libraries began to work with the Entrepreneurship Bootcamp for Veterans with Disabilities (EBV). This program supports veterans with disabilities who want to set up or expand their own business. The Texas A&M Libraries provide laptops, present on business research, provide research support, supply a year's worth of access to databases, and maintain LibGuides. The librarians want to help the veterans to improve their business research skills so they are better equipped to continue to research on their own. [26]

Business information services are a good way to reach out to a new community of users and connect to other organizations with a similar purpose such as SCORE, which is a group of retired business people who consult with small businesses, the small business development centers, and so forth. These networks can lead to strong ties for the library and an understanding of what the library can do for its community.

SOCIAL MEDIA AS OUTREACH

Social media is a good way to reach individuals beyond the library. Carefully crafted and regular messages from the library can be developed into a successful outreach campaign. Kaya van Beynen and Camielle Swenson at the University of South Florida looked at the libraries' sites on Facebook and student-run Facebook sites. They found that the library sites on Facebook received some attention but not an overwhelming amount. An Association of Research Libraries (ARL) study showed that 36 percent of the libraries had less than 100 fans and 31 percent had 100 to 250 fans. The libraries used Facebook for marketing events, resources, and services, and to answer general library questions. The authors then turned their attention to a student-run Facebook site at the University of South Florida called "The Know It All's Guide to Knowing It All." This site welcomed students, faculty, and staff. The authors monitored the references to the libraries on the site. During one school year there were 77 and 331 likes in the fall and 69 posts and 507 likes in the spring. They noted that there were more questions in the fall. Based on their observations, the librarians made three recommendations. First, the libraries should post information at peak times such as the beginning of the semester, at midterms, and at the end of the semester. Second, the libraries should use photographs with their messages to attract more attention. Third, the librarians recommended accepting and facilitating peer-to-peer support, as the students liked to hear from other students and the responses they received were accurate.[27]

Libraries can reach out through social media to provide information to their users. A well-organized advocacy or educational campaign can be very successful. Ross Fuqua describes a successful advocacy project in Oregon where a group of libraries needed to get a five-year levy passed. Although the library could not advocate as such for the levy, a series of factual information statements were sent out by all the libraries involved on a weekly basis using Facebook and Twitter. This carefully organized campaign resulted in the levy being passed.

OUTREACH WITH LIBGUIDES

LibGuides are another way to reach out to the community. For example, the University of Illinois at Urbana-Champaign Music and Performance Arts Library reached out to the Krannert Center for the Performing Arts (KCPA) using LibGuides. The library created a LibGuide for each month of the KCPA's season where they listed library resources for the audience to explore both before and after specific performances.[28] Another example is Georgia Southwestern State University Library, which partnered with local arts organizations through LibGuides to highlight local concerts and other events. As a result these organizations and their members not only were able to keep up to date on relevant events but also knew more about the library and its resources.[29] LibGuides have endless possibilities, and these examples show how useful they are as an outreach tool.

CONCLUSION

These examples of outreach activities show the value of librarians from different types of libraries moving outside the library and probably outside their comfort zone to bring their knowledge and skills to bear on community issues and problems. By reaching out in this way, librarians can impact a whole new group of users and demonstrate the value of libraries and librarians. Once out of the library and working with groups and individuals, librarians can spend time understanding their issues and problems in depth and anticipate their information needs; as a result, they can provide many more library resources. It is outreach that makes it possible to better understand the community information needs that libraries can address.

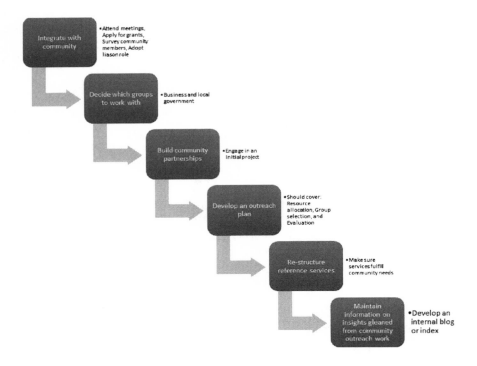

Figure 5.3.

NOTES

1. Colbe Galston et al., "Community Reference: Making Libraries Indispensable in a New Way," *American Libraries* 43, nos. 5/6 (2012): 46.

2. Michelle Lee, "Reference on the Road," *Library Journal* 138, no. 18 (2013): 18.

3. Galston et al., "Community Reference"; Lee, "Reference on the Road," 18–20.

4. Galston et al., "Community Reference."

5. Ibid.

6. "Imagine JCPL: A New Model for Library Service in Jefferson County," January 2012. Published for internal use by the Jefferson County Public Library.

7. Report provided in a management class.

8. Katelyn Angell and Eamon Tewell, "Collaborating for Academic Success: A Tri-Institutional Information Literacy Program for High School Students," *Public Services Quarterly* 9, no. 1 (2013): 1–19.

9. Matthew Lighthart and Creedence Spreder, "Partners in Lifelong Learning," *Knowledge Quest* 42, no. 4 (2014): 32–37.

10. Carrie Rogers-Whitehead, Lorelei Rutledge, and Jacob Reed, "Utah Accessible Tutorials: Creating a Collaborative Project Between a Public and Academic Library," *Collaborative Librarianship* 7, no. 2 (2015): 79–83.

11. Robert J. Engeszer et al., "Evolution of an Academic-Public Library Partnership," *Journal of the Medical Library Association* 104, no. 1 (2016): 62–66.

12. Sarah Lawton, "Drawing in the Community for Reference Services at Wilkinson Public Library in Telluride, Colorado," in *Reference Renaissance: Current and Future Trends*, ed. Marie L. Radford and R. David Lankes (New York: Neal-Schuman Publishers, 2010): 255–56.

13. Erin E. Meyer, "Low-Hanging Fruit: Leveraging Short-Term Partnerships to Advance Academic Library Outreach Goals," *Collaborative Librarianship* 6, no. 3 (2015): 112–20.

14. Susan Anderson, "Library Collaboration Index: Documenting the Reach in Outreach," *Indiana Libraries* 33, no. 2 (2014): 7–10.

15. Steven J. Bell, "Who Needs a Reference Desk?" *Library Issues: Briefings for Faculty and Administrators* 27, no. 6 (2007): 1–4.

16. David Shumaker, "The Embedded Librarians," *Online* 36, no. 4 (2012): 24–27.

17. Jerremie Clyde and Jennifer Lee, "Embedded Reference to Embedded Librarianship: 6 Years at the University of Calgary," *Journal of Library Administration* 51, no. 4 (2011): 389–402.

18. Catherine Essinger and Irene Ke, "Outreach: What Works?" *Collaborative Librarianship* 5, no. 1 (2013): 52–58.

19. Clyde and Lee, "Embedded Reference," 400.

20. Ibid., 389–402.

21. Paulita Aguilar et al., "Reference as Outreach: Meeting Users Where They Are," *Journal of Library Administration* 51, no. 4 (2011): 348.

22. Isabel D. Silver, "Outreach Activities for Librarian Liaisons," *Reference and User Services Quarterly* 54, no. 2 (2014): 8–14.

23. Patrick Griffis and Sidney Lowe, "Business Community Outreach: Exploration of a New Service Role in an Academic Environment," in *Leading the Reference Renaissance*, ed. Marie L. Radford, 161–68 (New York: Neal-Schuman, 2012).

24. Jared Hoppenfeld and Elizabeth Malafi, "Engaging with Entrepreneurs in Academic and Public Libraries," *Reference Services Review* 43, no. 3 (2015): 379–99.

25. Anne Therese Macdonald, "Dedicated Business Centers in Public Libraries," *Reference Services Review* 43, no. 3 (2015): 344–68.

26. Hoppenfeld and Malafi, "Engaging with Entrepreneurs."

27. Kaya van Beynen and Camielle Swenson, "Exploring Peer-to-Peer Library Content and Engagement on a Student-Run Facebook Group," *College and Research Libraries* 77, no. 1 (2016): 34–50.

28. Mandi Goodsett and Kirstin Dougan, "Community Outreach through LibGuides in Tyckoson," in *Reimagining Reference in the 21st Century*, ed. David A. Tyckoson and John G. Dove, 215–22 (West Lafayette, IN: Purdue University Press, 2015).

29. Ibid.

Chapter Six

Bringing Necessary Change to the Education and Training of Reference Librarians

The education and training of reference librarians has widened in scope from just answering the question correctly to an emphasis on the reference librarian's interaction with the patron. Further, digital technologies have increased both the diversity of information sources (e.g., electronic resources) and the ways that librarians can communicate with patrons (e.g., via instant message, chat, etc.). For this reason, librarians and prospective librarians must learn to work with patrons in a wide variety of settings and to meet their needs for information in whatever format is required. This chapter focuses on the education and training of librarians to provide reference and information services. It includes library school students and practitioners taking continuing education courses. Training includes not only providing information about reference and reference services but also allowing the students or practitioners a chance to practice their skills. To be discussed in this chapter are issues of approachability, verbal communication, listening, understanding the question, searching, follow-up, knowledge of sources, technology skills, information-literacy skills and understanding the research process, evaluation and assessment of sources, collaboration, customer service, the user experience, and marketing awareness.

In past decades, reference librarians have thought that answering reference questions correctly constituted the most important element of their jobs. However, research has demonstrated that other elements are just as, if not more, important to achieving patron satisfaction than providing a correct answer. Researchers such as Catherine Ross, Kirsti Nielsen, and Marie Radford discuss how librarian behavior influences whether the patron even ap-

proaches the librarian and if the patron would return to the same librarian.[1]
Findings from this research resulted in a changing approach to reference
service that continues in the present day as librarians become more patron
oriented and concentrate as much on developing a relationship with the patron as on the information resources. It is important for the librarian to have
enough time to work with the patron, thus making a good case for consultation services.

Two sets of guidelines for reference practice and competencies have been
developed by the Reference and User Services Association (RUSA) of the
American Library Association (ALA): "Guidelines for Behavioral Performance of Reference and Information Service Providers" and "Professional
Competencies for Reference and Patron Services Librarians."[2] The "Guidelines" resource outlines how librarians should interact with patrons during
the reference interview. It includes general guidelines and ones specific for
in-person and remote reference interactions. The guidelines are divided into
five main areas: visibility/approachability, interest, listening/inquiring,
searching, and follow-up.[3] The "Professional Competencies" resource discusses the competencies needed by reference librarians, which include access
(responsiveness, organization and design of service, critical thinking, and
analysis); knowledge base (environmental scanning, application of knowledge, dissemination of knowledge, and active learning); marketing/aware-
ness/informing (assessment, communication and outreach, and evaluation);
collaboration (relationships with patrons, relationships with colleagues, relationships within the profession, and relationships beyond the library and the
profession); and evaluation and assessment of resources and services (patron
needs, information services, information resources, service delivery, information interfaces, and information service providers).[4] The "Professional
Competencies" resource thus broadens the scope of reference-based considerations for practitioners by expanding the range of competencies beyond the
more basic considerations discussed in the "Guidelines."

Several studies build on these resources by asking practicing librarians
what competencies they feel are needed for reference work. An international
study of the most important reference competencies in thirteen countries,
which divided the competencies by general, technical, and personal/interper-
sonal skills, revealed that the highest-ranked general skills were search skills,
knowledge of online resources, and customer service; the highest-ranked
technical skills were online searching and knowledge of and facility with
social media; and the highest-ranked personal skills were verbal communication, listening, and approachability.[5] Another study by Mary Jordan of public
librarians rated the following skills as most important: online searching, verbal communication, customer service, listening, and approachability.[6] Two
different surveys with such similar results says a great deal about what skills
are needed to work effectively as a reference librarian, namely, the ability to

communicate with both colleagues and patrons, provide excellent customer service, and have good searching skills, particularly online. This chapter breaks down these results by general, technical, and personal-interpersonal skills,[7] and discusses how librarians can learn the skills and competencies related to each.

SKILLS AND COMPETENCIES

The remainder of the chapter overviews the following skills and competencies:

- Verbal communication and approachability (personal/interpersonal)
- Listening (personal/interpersonal)
- Understanding the question (personal/interpersonal)
- Searching (general; technical)
- Follow-up (personal/interpersonal)
- Knowledge of sources (general)
- Technology skills (technical)
- Information literacy skills and understanding the research process (personal/interpersonal; technical; general)
- Evaluation and assessment of sources (general)
- Collaboration (personal/interpersonal)
- Marketing awareness (general)
- Customer service (personal/interpersonal)

Verbal Communication and Approachability

We live in a fast-paced society where people expect to have instant responses to their information requests. Recent information behavior studies of library patrons denote timeliness as a key factor in determining satisfaction.[8] Yet certain reference questions require time to answer that may exceed the patron's expectations. In these situations, good customer service proves essential. Patrons must be confident that at the end of the time spent with the librarian, they will have some resources to begin their project or answer their information need. Where patrons once were content with minimal assistance and service, such as being pointed to the appropriate section of the stacks or being shown how to find a useful database, now their expectations are higher. Patrons expect assistance quickly, presented in a way that meets their needs, and delivered in the way they want it. These expectations signify that reference librarians must go beyond the basics and help the patron in a substantial way, while contending with high expectations related to the timeliness of the service.

To go beyond the basics, the librarian should take the first step of verbal communication with the patron and approachability. This step is taken for granted by many but in fact proves most important. Students and practitioners must understand that the librarian should appear friendly and ready to assist the patron. If the librarian appears busy and uninterested in the patron's information need, the patron may not want to continue with the librarian. Some of the traits that the librarian must display in the beginning of the reference encounter are eye contact, open body language, and a willingness to help.[9] When providing virtual reference services (VRS) it is important that the librarian acknowledge the patron's question as soon as possible, indicate that he or she is ready to help, and maintain contact so the patron knows that the librarian is searching for information. Librarians must also learn to listen carefully to the problem posed by patrons and be certain that they understand the question. Nothing we do after that can be effective if we fail at this first step. Studies have shown that more than any knowledge of technology or even collections, the need for excellent communication skills is paramount in any encounter with the patron.[10]

In an effort to provide equality of service, librarians have traditionally given an unwavering, basic level of service to all patrons. They would try to understand the question and help the patron to get started in a general way but leave it up to the patron to find the material he or she needed. This basic

Figure 6.1.   Librarian helping the patron at the point of need.

level of service, replicated across all patron groups, probably met few actual patron needs. Many library patrons need more extensive assistance depending on whether they use the library often or whether they seldom use it. For instance, when librarians assist patrons in beginning their search for needed information, they guide them to appropriate sources. This guidance may just mean identifying the appropriate database and subject terms. In other cases, it may mean helping patrons select appropriate articles and other resources based on the librarian's knowledge of them. In either case, the librarian must encourage patrons to let them know when more assistance is needed. For this reason, training must include learning to judge patrons' needs as an important first step in assisting them and include this judgment as a step of the reference interview. While this step does require more time from the librarian, it can also save the patrons time in the long term by providing them with quality resources relevant to their information need from the outset.

Not every subject area is one that the librarian knows well. So librarians must become facile at fielding questions and responding to subject requests outside of their areas of expertise. This facileness can be accomplished by turning to another librarian with more knowledge of the subject area or making the patron part of the librarian's team in identifying appropriate subject terminology and helping to determine the level of material needed. Most patrons are happy to work with the librarian since even if the librarian is not familiar with the subject area of the question, he or she is still an expert at identifying appropriate library resources.

Importance of Communication and Listening in the Reference Interview

Although librarians know the importance of the reference interview, it is interesting to see the emphasis on verbal communication and listening in the two studies mentioned at the beginning of the chapter.[11] The reference interview is a way for the librarian to gather information about the patron's information needs and develop rapport. Conducted properly, the reference interview will help the librarian understand the nature of the patron's information need and what the patron intends to do with the information. As the previous section outlines, there is a big difference in a patron's information needs depending on the context. The patron may want information to do an actual project or may be writing a paper on the concept. The kind of material needed for each situation will differ, hence the importance of understanding the context of the information request instead of just the subject.

Librarians need to develop good interview skills to assist the patron. To achieve this competency, the librarian should practice interview techniques so that the reference interview will seem natural when working with a patron. Specifically, it is useful to practice posing questions in several different ways depending on the situation at hand. Questions should be open ones so that patrons can easily follow-up and further explain what they are trying to do. For example, the librarian might ask, "Can you tell me more about your topic and how you intend to use the information?" Closed questions can move the interview in entirely wrong directions since the choices the librarian gives the patron may be misleading. For example, the librarian may ask, "Do you want information on China, the country, or china plates?" Neither of these choices may be the one the patron wants, which can leave the patron confused as to how to describe his or her information. Librarians should also practice the interview in a chat/instant messaging (IM) situation since many interviews are now conducted online. Librarians must carefully think out their questions to strike a balance between getting the most information possible from the patrons without seeming to ask too many questions. Clarifying questions should be used. These questions allow the patron to do most of the talking and make sure that the librarian remains on track in addressing the patron's information need, rather than imposing a need on the patron.

Understanding the Information Need

It is very easy to get only half of the story when the librarian talks to a patron. Patrons are trying to tell the librarian their information need in a way that they think the librarian wants to hear it. But sometimes they forget some important details so it is absolutely crucial that the student or practitioner learn how to follow-up the patron's explanation with a clarifying question. Even something as straightforward as "I need information on Chicago" can mean many things. The patron might want maps of Chicago, a list of places to visit, or a guide to interesting architecture. Each of these requests is different, yet the initial question did not include any of this information. A second question such as, "Could you tell me more about what kind of information on Chicago you need?" can clarify the patron's information need and help the librarian to find information that fulfills this need. The same clarification is required during the online interview, perhaps even more so given the brevity of expression within specific communication media, such as text or instant messaging. The librarian must read the information submitted carefully and ask a follow-up question to be sure that the reference query is understood. Patrons are often timid about saying that their question has not been answered so it is up to the librarian to ask in different ways if the patron is satisfied with the information. The patron should also be invited to return for additional information at the conclusion of the reference interview.

The key to performing a successful reference interview is understanding the question. Each word and sentence from patrons conveys information about their need for assistance. They are trying their best to convey their information need and the librarian must use all of what they are saying to understand how to help them. Sometimes the way patrons express themselves is rather subtle so the librarian must listen carefully and ask a follow-up question or two. Both in-person and virtual interviews require the same attention to detail. At some point the librarians will also want to rephrase the question to be sure they understand it correctly before beginning the search.

Searching

Searching skills are often listed as the most important competency for librarians after customer service. Much of the searching completed by patrons before visiting the reference desk is very superficial and often involves just using Google, which does not always identify the best resources. The librarian's in-depth knowledge of searching makes it possible to do advanced searching and uncover resources not necessarily identified in a more basic search. It is important that students and practitioners understand that searching cannot begin until the librarian has a good idea of the patron's information need. Trying to search with a vague idea of this need will not produce the kind of information that will satisfy the patron. Instead, the librarian needs to know the quantity, level, and format of information needed. This knowledge is required given that it will influence the search strategies used by the librarian, as well as the databases to be consulted. Searching involves knowing about the Boolean operators, which help to narrow and refine the search, and the subject terms used. Some databases use the Library of Congress subject headings while others use their own well-developed thesauri. Examples of databases with their own thesauri are ERIC, PsycINFO, and MEDLINE. Librarians working with patrons will want to help the patrons to identify the right terminology, narrow or broaden the search when necessary, understand how the search was done and how to continue searching on their own, and evaluate the resources found.

Follow-Up

The reference interview does not end after the patron has been provided with resources. According to the RUSA "Guidelines," "The librarian is responsible for determining if the patron is satisfied with the results of the search and referring the patron to other sources including those not available through the local library."[12] The follow-up is very important yet sometimes the most neglected part of the interview. Without follow-up the librarian cannot be sure that the patron is completely satisfied with the information received. Follow-up can be achieved by the librarian providing the patrons with a business card and encouraging them to be in touch if they need more information. However, some patrons are too timid to come back and ask for more information. In these cases, the librarian needs to follow-up with the

Figure 6.2. Students practicing searching.

patrons via phone, chat, or e-mail, or tell them verbally that they are welcome to come back and ask for further assistance. The librarian can perform follow-up by asking patrons for their e-mail or by providing a business card. Patrons also may not know that the library can get resources from other libraries if the patron is willing to wait. This information should be communicated by the librarian before ending the reference interview.

Knowledge of Sources

To provide information services effectively, librarians must be knowledgeable of the sources available to them and aware of other sources that are considered useful but may not be in their library or accessible there. The RUSA "Professional Competencies" guidelines frame access competencies as "the ability to identify documents through a knowledge of bibliography and indexing, the ability to identify and provide solutions that minimize cognitive and physical barriers to access and the ability to assess for individual patrons materials that will provide the appropriate level of linguistic and conceptual access."[13]

Librarians should have in-depth source knowledge, especially of electronic resources. This knowledge will help librarians to make the right decisions regarding specific databases to search. Databases are not all alike or even similar. They usually index and provide the articles for a group of journals and newspapers that have been carefully selected with some particular goal in mind. Some databases may include other material such as conference papers, research reports, dissertations, or government documents. For example, Public Affairs Information Service (PAIS) International indexes not only journal and newspaper articles but also government documents, books, gray literature, and research and conference reports on government, politics, public policy, and international relations. It is also international in scope. Educational Resources Information Center (ERIC) includes articles, research reports, conference papers, technical reports, books, and theses and dissertations on education, library science, psychology, and so forth. Based on the patron's information need, the librarian can make educated inferences of the types of sources the patron may wish to consult. For this reason, knowing what the patron can expect to find in a database is extremely useful. It is also useful for the librarian to know the level of material indexed within the database or index. Using this knowledge, the librarian can indicate to patrons whether the consulted resource is appropriate for the research they are doing. Some publishers produce several versions of an index/database for different audiences. They may have different versions for public and academic libraries, and even more than one version for a type of library depending on its size. Along with knowing the level of material indexed, it is also important to determine the available formats of indexed material. Although the resources used by libraries are rapidly changing, at this point it is still important to know what resources are only available in print and whether the information they contain can be found online. For some research areas, print sources may still be useful, especially in the humanities. The studies of practicing librarians mentioned earlier in the chapter all suggest the need for librarians to still know print resources as well as electronic ones.

To train librarians to know the breadth, depth, and format of available resources, training should include providing a great deal of information and practice using indexes and databases that are commonly used. The librarian must have an in-depth understanding of the differences in indexes and databases on the same subject and why one is used in some situations and not in others. A sound knowledge of which sources are heavily consulted by subject area is key to providing assistance, since the patrons may not be aware of the various sources available to them and therefore depend on the librarian to recommend databases or other sources that will be helpful within a specific information-seeking context.

Table 6.1.

Skill	In person	Virtually	Examples
Verbal communication and approachability	Librarians indicate that they are willing and eager to help the patrons.	Librarians acknowledge question as soon as possible and indicate their willingness to help.	In person: makes eye contact with patron approaching the reference desk and smiles at them. Virtually: "Hello, I am the reference librarian on call and am ready to answer your question."
Listening	Determining the context of the information request.	Same as in person. This determination is even more essential given the limited interpersonal cues.	"Can you tell me more about your topic and how you intend to use the information?"
Understanding the question	Follow-up with clarifying questions to make sure that the context of the information request is understood. It is important to understand how much information is needed, the level of information needed, and the format required.	Same as in person	"Around how many information sources are you looking to end up with?" "How many pages of reading are you looking to end up with?" "When do you need all of this information by?" "What is your level of knowledge on the subject?" "What is your preferred format(s) for the information sources returned?"
Knowledge of sources	Librarians must have in-depth knowledge of electronic sources, including the level of material indexed by the source and available formats of the source.	Same as in person	"Based on what you've told me, I suggest we search the following database, which has journal articles on this subject, available electronically, which you stated is your preferred format. In addition, this database presents articles written for individuals who

Component	In person	Virtual	Script
			have a basic understanding of the material, which matches your expressed basic level of understanding of the subject."
Searching	Librarians use knowledge of Boolean operators and subject headings to complete the searches. Librarians should also use the searching as a teaching moment to demonstrate to the patrons how to identify the right terminology, narrow or broaden the search when necessary, understand how the search was done, understand how to continue on their own, and evaluate the resources found.	Same as in person. In addition, the librarians may want to share screens with the patrons to discuss the search process, or at least communicate their search strategies. They will also want to indicate to the patrons when they are searching for information.	In person: "I am searching the database using the following search terms. Here are some of the results. Do you think these results are too narrow, too broad, or just right?" Virtually: "I am now going to search for information on this topic. This search may take a few minutes, so I will communicate my progress with you as it progresses [*time elapses*]. I searched the following database, which has journal articles on this subject, using the following search terms. Here are some of the results. Do you think these results are too narrow, too broad, or just right?" "I will now share my screen with you, so you can see how I am performing the search. I am searching the database using the following search terms. Here are some of the results. Do you think these results are too narrow, too broad, or just right?"
Customer service	Librarians must communicate with and listen to the patrons. The librarians must also be approachable. Other hallmarks	Same as in person.	"I will now show you how to search the database yourself, if you wish to search for more sources later, on your own."

	of customer service are negotiated within the specific library.		
Information literacy and understanding the research process	Provide enough information so that the patrons can find the information on their own.	Same as in person	"We also offer a class on how to search databases related to your topic of interest. It is offered every Wednesday at 5:00 p.m."
Technology skills	Librarians need to possess the following: online searching capabilities, software troubleshooting, familiarity with chat/instant messaging, software troubleshooting, and knowledge of how to develop web pages, how to use social media, what discovery systems can and cannot do, and what citation management software exists and how to evaluate this software.	Same as in person. Also how to capture and present data and images from the both web and databases to answer questions.	In person: "You said as part of the reference interview that you want to cite the sources we selected in APA style for a paper. I would recommend the following software to manage your citations and will now show you how this software works." Virtually: "I took the following screenshot of the database so that you can see the recommended search terms over on the left-hand side. You will note that the database has suggested both broader and narrower search terms to use if you are not satisfied with this list of initial results."
Evaluation and assessment of sources	Librarians must work closely with the patrons to determine how to evaluate and assess the sources retrieved based on the context of the patrons' information need.	Same as in person	"Since you also indicated that you want very recent resources, I recommend that we look at the following database, which offers preprints of articles."
Collaboration	The librarian should collaborate with the patron, other librarians, and outside experts, when necessary.	Same as in person	"You may also wish to speak with our subject specialist if you desire more in-depth information about this topic."

Follow-up	Determining if the patrons are satisfied, referring them to other sources that might not be held by the library (if applicable), letting the patrons know that the librarians can obtain resources from other libraries if the patrons are willing to wait (if applicable), and providing contact information for the librarian	Same as in person	"Are you satisfied with the sources we have come up with during the reference interview? Are there any other areas that we should cover? Keep in mind that I can obtain sources for you held by other libraries, but you may have to wait a few days to access these sources. Would you be interested in pursuing these other sources? Do you have any other information needs that I can address? Please take my [business card or e-mail address] and get in touch with me if you have any follow-up questions or new questions."
Marketing awareness	Consists of assessment, communication, outreach and evaluation	Same as in person	"Thank you again for using our reference services. Would you mind taking a brief survey to indicate your satisfaction with the services I provided for you today?"

Technology Skills Needed

Although there can be too much emphasis on technology in training, librarians must have basic technology skills to work with the public. Laura Saunders reported that the skills needed by librarians include online searching capabilities, software troubleshooting, and familiarity with chat/instant messaging.[14] Jordan also mentioned online searching skills.[15] Online searching capabilities go beyond basic searching skills to the use of advanced search engines requiring more in-depth searching knowledge (e.g., Boolean searching and subject headings). This need for advanced knowledge is particularly true with subject-specific databases such as PsycINFO. Software troubleshooting may include knowledge of chat/IM, social media, blogging, wikis, texting, RSS, and more. Further, librarians providing chat, e-mail, and text reference need to know how to capture and present data and images from both the web and databases to answer questions. Librarians must also understand how to develop web pages and use social media, as well as what discovery systems can and cannot do, what citation management software exists, and how to evaluate this software. Becoming comfortable with new technology is thus necessary to meet patron needs and expectations as well as continuing to monitor new developments in technology that might be usefully applied to library services.

Evaluation of Sources and Materials

Before evaluation, students and practitioners need to learn how to understand the information needs of the patron and how they intend to use the information. Only with an in-depth understanding of the patron's information needs and intended uses can the librarian evaluate information found to see if it meets the patron's expectations. This understanding can be achieved by working carefully with the patron. It is no longer enough to simply gather a large quantity of information hoping that the patron will find a few useful pieces. Instead, librarians should be using their knowledge of information sources in a subject area to guide patrons to the best sources of information for their needs. This knowledge may result in finding resources with different points of view, that are peer reviewed, and that reflect the latest research in a rapidly changing subject area. It may also mean knowing where new information in a given field is being published, which may not be located in databases (e.g., preprints and blogs).

Customer Service

All libraries acknowledge the importance of customer service. But how do we define this service, and is what we provide adequate? Sometimes politeness is viewed as customer service. However, while politeness is important, it is not the heart of customer service. Instead, customer service can be defined as "the fact of treating customers in a polite and helpful way, which is considered an important part of running a good business."[16] However, definitions of customer service, including which elements comprise this service, will vary by library. For this reason, libraries should define customer service for their staff members so they will have some parameters within which to work. The staff needs to know the degree of service expected. Do we expect staff to go to the shelves with patrons? Do we expect the staff to help the patron find appropriate articles in a database or simply show the patron the database? Many studies of customer service within reference contexts mention verbal communication as an important skill. Although the combination of verbal communication and listening fall into more than one category of important reference services provided, they comprise a significant part of customer service. Communicating with the patron as well as listening is indeed necessary to provide good service. Someone who is just polite but in a hurry to get rid of the patron will not win any points for customer service. Another key facet of customer service is approachability. If a librarian looks as if he or she does not want to talk to anyone, the patron will not approach the librarian and ultimately any efforts to provide customer service will not have a chance to be extended. Finally customer service means thinking ahead of what the patron wants but has not yet articulated.

Information Literacy Skills and Understanding the Research Process

Instruction has become a big part of a librarian's job, especially in academic libraries but in other types as well. It is not enough to assist patrons in finding information; it is also necessary to teach them how to find materials and information on their own. Information-literacy training should include the various instructional models such as working with different types of patrons, presenting in various contexts (e.g., face-to-face and virtually) and for different purposes. An instruction session may include a librarian just doing a short presentation for a class or can be more in depth, such as the librarian organizing a group activity for students to learn a particular skill. Here, it is important to tailor the presentation to the group as generic presentations do not often meet the patrons' needs. Presenting at the point of need can be more useful and provide more helpful information. For example, the teacher might ask the librarian to make a presentation just as the students are beginning to do research for a paper. Librarians also need to learn to evaluate what level of instruction is needed in a particular situation and adjust their presentations accordingly.

In addition to group information-literacy classes, one-to-one library instruction is needed. Such in-depth interaction is important to help the patron understand the research process so the patron can replicate it the next time. Key topics covered during one-on-one instruction include refining the subject, identifying materials, developing the topic, citing the information used correctly, and preparing the final paper. There are also other areas where librarians can provide one-on-one instruction, such as copyright issues and finding appropriate places to publish an article.

Collaboration

The RUSA "Professional Competencies" guidelines discuss the role of collaboration in the reference process.[17] Collaboration can be with patrons, other librarians, external experts, internal departments, or outside organizations. In any case, the role of collaboration is an important one; since no one can have all the knowledge required to serve an extensive patron base, it makes good sense that working with others will enhance the work of librarians. Collaborating with a patron may mean that the results will be more precise. Collaborating with a librarian colleague may mean finding other resources that assist in locating what the patron needs. Collaborating with an outside expert can provide other insights into a particular field of study. And finally collaborating with internal departments or outside organizations can help the library accomplish projects that would not have been easy to accomplish on its own.

Marketing

The RUSA "Professional Competencies" guidelines define a marketing plan as "an aspect of strategic planning that is a promotional mechanism by which goals, objectives and strategies can be measured in a quantitative manner."[18] The guidelines suggest assessment, communication, and outreach and evaluation as key elements comprising a sound marketing plan.[19] Assessment can be measured by using statistics, surveys, focus groups, and observation depending on what the library wants to know. Sometimes it is useful to do assessment before and after a marketing event to better understand what has or has not been accomplished. For example, if the library has an event designed to attract new patrons, it can use information on how many people attended and perhaps survey-based results. Communication and outreach can be measured using electronic media and print. For a detailed discussion of assessment and evaluation, see chapter 7, "Keeping Up with Change through More Effective Assessment."

Marketing is key to successful library service. Because more and more patrons turn to virtual reference, they may have less knowledge as to what resources are available from the library and what services are available. The library must use many means of communication including newsletters, blogs, social media, and presentations to inform its patrons of its potential.

Management and Supervisory Skills

Since most library positions have some management and supervisory responsibilities, students and practitioners must learn about management and supervisory tasks. Training will assist in future situations where they may be asked to schedule reference services, prepare the reference budget, hire and train staff, manage online resources, and even design and maintain the website. What was once a job that mostly involved reference service and collection development can now be one that results in constant multitasking. For this reason, a management course is an essential part of a library science curriculum.

Packaging the Information Sources

Although this chapter has discussed the importance of the librarian in providing reference services that fulfill the patron's information needs and expectations for use, often it will be appropriate for the librarian to make an initial selection of material to help the patron get started. This service is not always necessary but in some situations will be expected and welcomed. For instance, a librarian working with a faculty member may point him or her to certain resources for teaching a new course or researching within a new subject area. To get the patron started, the librarian must decide how to present information in an objective way and provide enough information to get the patron started. Such information might be a list of resources, which might have one-sentence descriptions or be organized by subject area. Depending on the type of library, there are different expectations as to what the librarian should provide. However, getting the patron started by identifying some key articles and other information is not an unusual service. One way to learn how to get the patron started is to practice developing LibGuides on various subjects, which will provide guidance to the patron by listing the best sources on a topic.

Key competencies for new librarians are the following:

- Searching skills
- Knowledge of information sources
- Communication and listening skills
- Knowledge of all aspects of the reference interview
- Knowledge of technology
- Customer service skills
- Awareness of marketing opportunities

- Ability to develop collaborative relationships

CONCLUSION

Training a reference librarian is a very complicated process since the skills needed are now very diverse. They range from having a public service attitude and thinking outside the box to reaching out to new audiences and working in a collaborative manner. Knowledge of how to work with patrons and of important information sources are both needed. It also requires technology skills and an ability to teach and communicate information clearly. Training will be a multifaceted job and require those who want to be reference librarians to absorb a great deal of information.

NOTES

1. Catherine Sheldrick Ross, Kirsti Nielsen, and Marie L. Radford, *Conducting the Reference Interview*, 2nd ed. (New York: Neal-Schuman, 2009).

2. "Guidelines for Behavioral Performance of Reference and Information Service Providers," Reference and User Services Association, accessed July 13, 2016, http://www.ala.org/; Jo Bell Whitlatch et al., "Professional Competencies for Reference and Patron Services Librarians," Reference and User Services Association, January 26, 2003, http://www.ala.org/.

3. "Guidelines for Behavioral Performance."

4. Whitlatch et al., "Professional Competencies."

5. Laura Saunders, "Culture and Competencies: A Multi-country Examination of Reference Service Competencies," *Libri* 63, no. 1 (2013): 33–46.

6. Mary Wilkins Jordan, "Reference Desks in Public Libraries: What Happens and What to Know," *Reference Librarian* 55, no. 3 (2014): 196–211.

7. Saunders, "Culture and Competencies."

8. Lynn Silipigni Connaway et al., "'I Always Stick with the First Thing That Comes Up on Google . . .': Where People Go for Information, What They Use, and Why," in *The Library in the Life of the Patron: Engaging with People Where They Live and Learn*, comp. Lynn Silipigni Connaway (Dublin, OH: OCLC Research, 2015), 173, http://www.oclc.org/.

9. "Guidelines for Behavioral Performance."

10. Taryn Resnick, Ana Ugaz, and Nancy Burford, "E-resource Helpdesk into Virtual Reference: Identifying Core Competencies," *Reference Services Review* 38, no. 3 (2010): 347–59.

11. Jordan, "Reference Desks"; Saunders, "Culture and Competencies."

12. "Guidelines for Behavioral Performance."

13. Whitlatch et al., "Professional Competencies."

14. Saunders, "Culture and Competencies."

15. Jordan, "Reference Desks."

16. *Cambridge Dictionary*, sv "customer service," accessed July 25, 2016, http://dictionary.cambridge.org/.

17. Whitlatch et al., "Professional Competencies."

18. Ibid.

19. Ibid.

Chapter Seven

Keeping Up with Change through More Effective Assessment

In our intensely competitive world it is not just enough to provide basic services. Librarians must also monitor how they are doing to improve this service and to be accountable to their patrons and to their funding body. It is becoming routine to survey patrons frequently, hold focus groups, and find other ways to document the reference service being provided and whether it is meeting user needs. An important part of developing any library service is therefore assessment and evaluation. Although evaluation and assessment are often used interchangeably, "evaluations are designed to document the level of achievement that has been attained."[1] Grades are one example of an evaluation. Evaluative data tends to be quantitative. "Assessment, on the other hand, is focused on measuring a performance, work product, or skill in order to offer feedback on strengths and weaknesses and to provide direction for improving future performance."[2] We often talk about assessment of information-literacy classes, and assessment data tends to be qualitative. Decision making should be based on some assessment or evaluation. This chapter will explore specific examples of how librarians can get feedback from their patrons to document the work they are doing and to obtain information that will help them to improve their services or programs. Various methods of doing assessment and evaluation will be discussed. The ways that libraries evaluate and assess their services using both qualitative and quantitative methods will be described as well as guidelines on how to develop and administer each evaluation method.

Libraries use evaluation and assessment to find out how they are doing. They may want to know about the number of resources being used (quantitative information) or about user satisfaction, the quality of service being provided, and other user needs that have not been addressed (qualitative information). Both quantitative and qualitative information can be useful, and both measures should be included since they complement each other. The library may have a positive evaluation based on its high circulation numbers but a negative assessment based on user descriptions of the collection as dated. One would not be able to pinpoint areas of strength and weakness relative to a library's performance without considering each element from a series of qualitative and quantitative lenses.

For this reason, evaluation and assessment need to be developed in relation to what the library wants to measure, including identification of appropriate instruments to collect the data and appropriate methods to analyze the data. The results of a well-thought-out evaluation and assessment plan can be used to show that the library is being accountable and that it is spending its money wisely. It can demonstrate its impact and relevance and that it is responding to the needs of its patrons. Depending on what is being assessed or evaluated, the library could ask one or more of the following questions:

1. How much or how many?
2. How economical?
3. How valuable?
4. How reliable or how accurate?
5. How well?
6. How courteous or how responsive?
7. How satisfied?[3]

Some of these questions can be answered internally by the library, particularly, How much? How many? and How economical? Others can be answered by the library and its patrons, that is, How valuable? How reliable or accurate? and How well? And yet others can be answered only by the patrons, that is, How courteous? How responsive? and How satisfied?[4]

For an example of how Peter Hernon's model is applied, consider the proposed evaluation and assessment of a library's reference services. We can first of all collect the data for "how much" reference is being done and "how many" questions are being posed and answered. With these two data points, we can then calculate the cost per question answered (how economical). "How valuable" includes both the cost and the benefits to the patron. Both costs and benefits could be derived from a series of measures, such as the time taken to retrieve relevant information and the patron's satisfaction with this information. "How reliable or accurate" can be a joint judgment between the library and the patron, and "how well" combines measures from accuracy and promptness to completeness that can again be derived by both the library and patron. The last three questions are the domain of the patron who must weigh in on courteousness, responsiveness, and satisfaction with the reference service they received. Various tools discussed in this chapter can be

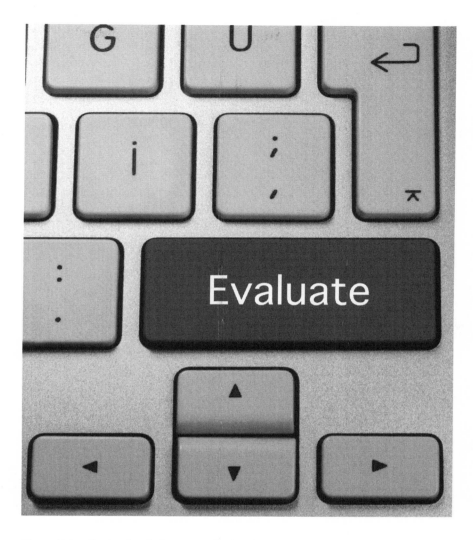

Figure 7.1. Evaluation is important in developing library service.

used to collect and analyze the defined scope of data and ultimately answer these questions. [5]

Statistics Gathering

Although statistics to compare peer libraries have been used for many years, they comprise only part of the evaluation. But it is still important to look at what statistics gathering can tell us and how statistics can be used. Statistics answer the following questions: How much? How many? And how economical? Many statistics are collected in libraries including circulation statistics, use of e-resources, interlibrary loan requests, and gate counts. Statistics can also be derived by counting the number of people visiting the library, reference requests, use of the website, reserve use, program attendance and collection information such as the number of titles in each subject area, the number of titles by format such as in the print collection and the e-resource collection, what changes are occurring in the acquisition of library resources, and so on. Each of these statistical categories can be further specified, such as breaking down the number of titles in the print collection to number of unique titles and number of duplicate titles.

Statistics is one way to demonstrate the value of the library and its services. Statistics can provide information about how much the library is being used and by how many people. It can also show from year to year whether the way the collection and services are being used is changing. For example, is the circulation of print materials going down and the use of e-resources rising? Are more people using audio and video resources? Are fewer print materials being purchased and more e-resources being purchased? What about reference statistics? Are the number of questions being asked by chat going up and in-person questions going down? There are many things that we can learn from statistics. But statistics themselves do not have all the answers and should be thought of as only one possible way to view an issue. For this reason, we have to think about the underlying reasons for producing the statistics. Are e-books not used enough because the patrons don't like e-books or because the selection does not meet their needs? Is the chat service not doing as well as it should because it does not appeal to the patrons, because they do not know about it, or because the hours of chat are too limited and do not meet user needs? Using statistics may serve as a good way to identify an initial issue, for example, e-books not being used enough, but other modes of data collection and analysis are required to explain why the issue is occurring.

One productive use of descriptive statistics is to count the number of reference questions asked. There are a number of statistical software packages available to count reference questions. They include Gimlet, Desk Tracker, and Libstats. Libstats moves beyond just quantitative information. In addition to collecting location, patron type, question type, time spent, and question format, it allows the librarian to add the question and its answer. This feature is very useful since the library now has some qualitative data that can be used to better understand who is using the library and the level of the questions. For instance, perhaps reference questions on the whole are declining but those asked are more involved. Question-and-answer data can also be used to develop staff training by identifying exemplary reference exchanges.

One of the ways to judge the value of the library is to analyze costs in relation to the services and programs provided.[6] This analysis is often referred to as ROI, or return on investment. It answers the question, How valuable? "An ROI makes possible such statements as 'for each dollar spent on the library, the community receives $_____ in benefits from library service.'"[7] ROI can be determined from the point of view of the library or from the point of view of the patron. Libraries can calculate ROI multiplying the quantity times the unit price. "If ten thousand articles were downloaded, and the library assigned a price of $15 per article, the value of use is $150,000."[8] Or if it were from the point of view of the patron, the library could post a value calculator on its website that the patrons could use to determine the value of library services relative to the potential costs incurred by the patron. An example of a value calculator can be found on the American Library Association website.[9]

Another example of how ROI can be calculated from the user point of view is by calculating SROI, or student return on investment, within academic libraries. Once again a value calculator is used to compare how much students pay as part of their fees for the library in relation to what the students say that the library is worth. An example is available from the West Florida Libraries.[10]

As previously stated, these statistics are only part of the picture. Statistics are quantitative, but in order to see the complete picture we must add qualitative data, collected using methods such as surveys, focus groups, interviews, observation, and usability studies, as well as methods such as action gap analysis. It is equally important to know if the way the library provides services is meeting the needs of the patrons. The collection can be large, but is it the right collection? The library continues to attract a large group of patrons, but could it provide other services that would attract a new group of patrons? These qualitative measures answer the following questions: How well? How responsive? How satisfied? And how reliable?

Surveys

Surveys are a concrete way of getting information from patrons, particularly large groups. By having the ability to collect information from larger groups, libraries can find out descriptive information about their patrons, such as demographic information, library use, impressions of the library, and level of satisfaction with the library. It is important to decide whether the library wants to survey a particular user group, such as students in an academic library or business people in a public library, or wants to open the survey to anyone who will answer it. This decision will affect the generality of the claims the library can make about its user base.

To gather data that is representative, the library should try to find a way to distribute the survey to get as large a response as possible, such as by handing it out in the library or placing it on the website. If obtaining a large, generalizable sample is not possible, the library can also do a planned sampling. Planned sampling strategies include stratified sampling, which involves identifying both the different types of patrons the library has and the specific proportion that each group comprises of the total patron population, and sampling a given number of patrons from each group using this proportion.

A good survey will have carefully developed questions that are easy to understand. It is important to consider the order of the questions. Many recommend putting the demographic questions at the end. Although the library can with some assistance develop a survey, it is often better to use a survey where the questions have already been tested such as LibQUAL+ offered through the Association of Research Libraries or LibSat from Counting Opinions (http://www.countingopinions.com/). LibQUAL+ measures user perceptions of service quality. LibSat can be available 24/7 so that patrons can continue to give the library feedback. The look of the survey is also important, and it should be free of spelling errors. If the survey has not been tested, it is a good idea to perform a pilot test using the survey to ensure that mistakes are corrected, to ensure that patrons can understand the questions being asked, and to confirm that the survey is collecting the data the library wants to measure. The results should be compiled with accuracy so there is no doubt as to the results. Often such accuracy can be achieved by performing validity testing, which varies based on whether qualitative or quantitative methods are used as well as the type of analysis employed. In any case, an explanation must be available as to the methodology used in reports of the findings.

Among the types of surveys are the following:

- A paper survey, which can be distributed in the library or mailed;
- A telephone survey; and
- A web-based survey.

Surveys can also be performed using software. For instance, Georgia State University piloted an evaluation program using iPads. They called it "guerilla-style assessment." They found the iPad very effective for short surveys. Further, students seemed to like using the iPad and were willing to do the survey, increasing the response rate. Also the portability of the iPad meant that the librarian could move around the library to find students to survey, increasing the variability of patrons surveyed. They tried various software because it is important to know how the software will impact how the survey can be done. For instance, certain software did not require an

Figure 7.2.   Online surveys are one way to collect information from patrons.

Internet connection to administer the survey, rendering it easier for the library to administer the survey in different locations.

Library patrons are not the only ones who should be surveyed about their perceptions of the library. It is also a good idea to find out how staff members view their role in customer service. Questions on a customer service questionnaire for staff members could include their impressions of how patrons are treated, whether patrons have to wait for service, whether the staff put the customer first, and what customer service changes the staff would suggest. The results of this survey can be compared with a library customer survey about whether they receive good service in the library. Discrepancies between these two surveys will give management information about any situation that needs to be corrected. It is important to work toward staff and patrons having the same priorities.

The following are guidelines for surveys:

1. Decide on what the library wants to learn from the survey and from the target audience.
2. Decide how the survey should be administered—in person, by mail, or online.
3. Develop questions carefully. Use mostly fixed-choice questions. Use neutral language.

4. Ask questions that will be useful once the results are available. Think in advance how the results will be used.

5. Try to keep the survey to no more than two pages to respect the patrons' time.

6. Pretest the survey on staff or a select group of patrons to be sure that the language is clear and that the responses are what are expected.

7. Decide how to distribute the survey. For example, it could be distributed in the library, on the library website, or by e-mail.

Focus Groups

Focus groups are a way to gain qualitative information from patrons about the library. They answer the questions "why?" and "how well?" They provide patrons with a chance to share views about the library and come up with new ideas that may be different than those of any one member of the group. For example, running focus groups is a good way to get information and new ideas about a particular service or collection. Focus groups tend to be small—six to ten members. The members of the focus group can be selected by the library so the library can select a group that reflects a certain area of interest or has something in common.

Once focus group members are selected, they engage in a structured discussion and respond to open-ended questions. A good moderator is an essential part of a focus group. The moderator needs to keep the discussion going without undue interference. It is not the role of the moderator to engage in the discussion, but it is the role of the moderator to encourage all participants to take part in the discussion. Therefore, the moderator must carefully enact his or her role as facilitator in mitigating individual contributors who may be dominating the conversation, while asking those who have not shared their opinions for further elicitation. The usefulness of the focus group is that it is free flowing and limited in its subject. These features allow for the introduction of new ideas and initiatives that may not be yielded using more structured methods, such as survey collection. Focus-group discussion can also be recorded so the library can review the results at a later date and follow up on good ideas. Results may or may not be generalizable to a larger group of patrons, depending on who is sampled and what the library wants to measure.

For example, a public library is thinking of expanding its services to the business community. A group of library patrons who are business people are invited to join a focus group to find out how they are presently using the library and what else the library could provide for them. The library has thought about increasing the business resources, offering workshops on areas of interest, or even one-to-one consultations. But they need more feedback before they move ahead. A focus group is a quick and easy way to get more information and opinions. Findings from the focus group can lead to more structured assessment and evaluation moving forward, such as a survey-based evaluation of business resources currently offered.

The following are guidelines for focus groups:

1. Select a good moderator who knows how to conduct a focus group and can remain neutral.
2. Choose the focus group participants carefully so they seem to be people who will work well together.
3. Be respectful of the participants' time since they are doing the library a favor.
4. Be sure the participants are comfortable. Offer refreshments, and make sure everyone is introduced.
5. Prepare the questions in advance. There can be open-ended questions and closed questions.
6. Keep the questions for the focus group in a specific area so that the group does not wander into other areas.
7. Emphasize that the results will not mention specific people's ideas so the participants have some assurance that there is a level of anonymity.
8. Keep the focus group to no more than ninety minutes.
9. Offer some feedback after the focus group if that seems appropriate.

Interviews

Interviews are a way to get very specific information from a limited number of people. Interviews can be used to supplement quantitative evaluation-based data. For instance, if the library is finding that a certain resource has experienced a decline of use, it might be worthwhile to ask patrons why before making the decision to remove the resource from the collection. Perhaps the resource still remains essential but to a specific subset of patrons. Interviews could be short and informal or could be longer and more formal. They can be structured, semistructured, or open. Structured means that the interview questions are all planned in advance. Semistructured means that part of the interview is planned in advance. Open means the interviewer and interviewee can talk freely about the subject at hand. Developing the interview protocol really depends on how much and what type of information is needed. Longer interviews will demand that the library hire someone to do the interviews or that a staff member is assigned as part of their duties to conduct the interviews because they are very time consuming. But if the library has a particular audience in mind and wants to know what they think, this can be quite useful.

The following are guidelines for interviews:

1. Have a particular purpose as to what kind of information the library wants to gain by doing interviews.
2. Select carefully the people to interview who are likely to respond positively to this opportunity to talk about the library. Tell them how the interview will help the library plan its services.
3. Make appointments and keep to the schedule. Tell the person in advance how long the interview will be. They are doing the library a favor to do this.
4. Take good notes or tape the interview if possible.

Usability Studies

Usability studies are often used to evaluate websites but can also be used to evaluate information systems, products, and technology. The idea of usability studies is to judge the satisfaction of the patron and the patrons' ability to easily understand how to perform basic tasks on whatever is being tested. Too many errors performed by the patrons involved in the study may mean that the product lacks ease of use. When completing usability studies, a certain number of patrons must be identified who are willing to spend time trying out the website or other technology to judge its usability.

A good usability study example is from Portland State University Library. Here the library had developed a new mobile website and needed to find out if it was "user-friendly and effective . . . on students' various mobile devices."[11] The authors take the reader step by step through the process that could be applied to any usability study of a website. This process involves the following steps:

1. Decide on the number of participants necessary to capture site behavior (generally between five and eight).
2. Ask participants to complete test scenarios based on key functional objectives of the specific program or piece of software.
3. Record participants' behaviors on the site as they complete the tasks.
4. Use techniques, such as the "think aloud" protocol, to elicit further information of user perceptions while completing the task. Just because a procedure was successfully completed does not indicate that the patron did not experience difficulty figuring out how to complete it.
5. Analyze data using a set of tested measures, such as efficiency or effectiveness, and make sure to establish validity of scoring using these measures by having more than one person analyze the data.

They found the mobile website to be mostly successful but did make some changes as a result of the usability study. These changes included rendering certain buttons and categories more visible on the site, as well as removing superfluous options.

Another usability study was that at the LSE (London School of Economics) Library. The library wanted to see how easy it was to use Summons Discovery System, which they called Library Search. They did a survey, direct observation, and a focus group. They found the direct observation particularly useful because it "allowed the team to observe which features patrons were prioritizing and to identify 'unknown unknowns'—instances when patrons may have thought they were using Library Search to its full potential but were actually missing features that might have increased the effectiveness of their search."[12] The authors said that the direct observation was so useful because it revealed a great deal that the patrons had not stated in the survey or focus group. It gave the library a more accurate idea of how the patrons were using Library Search.

Benchmarking

"Benchmarking comparisons are usually based on time, cost and quality as measured against previous performance, others in the organization or profession, or the best in that class."[13] Benchmarking can be divided into three categories. Internal benchmarking is where the performance of some task is compared with previous performances of the task within the organization over a period of time. Competitive benchmarking is where one library's performance is compared with peer libraries, institutions, or related organizations. Functional or comparative benchmarking is where the library looks at how others are accomplishing the same task. For example, a library could compare how it moves from one unit to another.[14] Benchmarking can provide a way to compare processes or tasks within a library or other organization or to compare between libraries and organizations. Some guidelines for benchmarking are the following:

1. Select a process for benchmarking.
2. Identify the steps involved in the process.
3. Gather the available data.
4. Look at how to do the process better.
5. Examine steps that could be eliminated.

Measuring Virtual Service

Measuring virtual service is an emerging area of interest as current virtual reference (VR) technologies change both in the services they provide and in the amount they are used, as well as the introduction of new VR technologies. Librarians may want to measure it separately to evaluate if it is meeting user needs. This could take the form of an online survey at the end of a chat session or an e-mail transaction. The library could then ask those filling out the survey if they would be willing to be interviewed.

But VR services are not the only services libraries provide virtually. It is also important to know the uses of other virtual resources provided, such as within the library website and among particular parts of the website, such as LibGuides. For example, Are library-created guides such as LibGuides well used? What about web-based tutorials? Are web-based forms well used?

Social Media

Social media such as Facebook and Twitter can also be useful in finding out what patrons think about the library and can supplement other data-collection methods, such as interviews. The library will not get a lot of information from social media, but comments from the public may give the library clues into issues that need resolving. Further, these comments may differ from those elicited using other methods due to the mode of the technology; for example, the user is not telling a librarian to his or her face, and the fact that patrons on social media may differ from those being surveyed, interviewed, and so forth, by the library. Complaints are more likely to pop up rather than compliments, but it is a good way to get some feedback that might not be elicited by these other data-collection methods.

Case Studies

The following case studies represent a combination of specific data-collection and analysis techniques described above. By combining methods, the libraries overviewed were able to derive rich results and findings that would not have been identified by any standalone method.

The University of Arizona libraries used several evaluation techniques to understand more about the usage and performance of their libraries' reference services. One thing the university wanted to determine was what questions were being asked and what level of staff was needed to answer them. One way to document these two measures is to count and analyze all questions received at the reference desk and by phone. To this end, the University of Arizona described "logging and analyzing questions" as one part of their data-collection method. For a specific period of time staff members recorded (in an Access database) each question that they answered, how long it took to answer the question, and if the question was referred to a subject specialist. Then the questions were analyzed by qualitatively coding them as one of six categories: reference, directional, technology use, technology problems, circulation questions, and questions about nonlibrary campus services.[15] The result of this study showed that most questions could be answered by students and trained generalists. Subject specialists were not used on the reference desks but were available for referrals.

The libraries also wanted information about user satisfaction. For this component of the study, they used a survey technique called "Customer Action Process" (CAP), which provided respondents with a list of reference service components available and asked patrons to indicate using the same list which were the most important, which organization did the best, and which were most in need of improvement. The list included a wide range of services such as "Help identifying articles and/or books for your research topic" and "Explaining the search process/showing how we get the answer."[16] The results were evaluated by counting the services identified as most important, best, or in need of improvement. A focus was placed on items that were ranked as most important but were not ranked highly in the other two categories.[17] These items suggested the ones that required immediate focus, such as providing alternate access to items the library does not currently own.

A second case study comes from the University of Calgary Libraries, which also did a study of usage of the libraries. They used volunteers at each reference desk to observe the number of questions, the length of time to answer the questions, and the types of questions. Observation took place over the fall and winter. The types of questions were qualitatively coded as directional, reference, technology, and referral. The study was meant to be a sampling only and thus could not be generalized to the overall library population. However, preliminary findings could be used to inform further more directed data collection about elements of reference services found to be particularly problematic. Based on these initial observations, the author stated that "some baseline data has been collected about how much time it takes to answer questions and the variety of activities that occur at the reference service desks. . . . Planning is currently underway to implement appropriate models for reference service delivery across a multifaceted information organization. . . . Reference is moving to more integrated, single-service desks, staffed by a mix of librarians and paraprofessionals."[18]

Evaluation and assessment are key to understanding how libraries and library services are doing. Unless we add these components to every project we will be missing that patron feedback that we need so much. We can have the best service in the world and yet miss what our patrons need. Thus attaining evaluation and assessment measures is an important, albeit time-consuming, step to take. Yet we cannot know if we are meeting user needs without adequate evaluation and assessment.

The following table depicts common differences between data-collection and data-analysis methods based on whether an evaluation or assessment is being made. It should be noted, however, that these differences are not abso-

Figure 7.3.   Assessment is important in understanding how the library is doing.

lute; rather, they represent methods that often characterize either evaluation or assessment.

Table 7.1.

	Data collection		Data analysis	
	Qualitative	*Quantitative*	*Qualitative*	*Quantitative*
Evaluation	Structured interviews	Surveys (close ended)	Deductive coding	Descriptive statistics
Assessment	Semistructured interviews; focus groups	Surveys (open ended)	Inductive coding	Inferential statistics

NOTES

1. Susan Starr, "Moving from Evaluation to Assessment," *Journal of the Medical Library Association*, 102, no. 4 (2014): 227.
2. Ibid.
3. Peter Hernon, Ellen Altman, and Robert E. Dugan, *Assessing Service Quality*, 3rd ed. (Chicago: American Library Association, 2015), 40–53.
4. Ibid., 49.
5. Ibid.
6. Ibid., 42.
7. Ibid., 43.
8. Ibid.
9. "Library Value Calculator," American Library Association, accessed November 3, 2016, http://www.ala.org/.

10. "Student Return on Investment (SROI)," Office of the Dean of Libraries, University of West Florida, last updated October 19, 2016, http://libguides.uwf.edu/.

11. Kimberly D. Pendell and Michael S. Bowman, "Usability Study of a Library's Mobile Website: An Example from Portland State University," *Information Technology and Libraries* 31, no. 2 (2012): 46.

12. Anna Grigson, Catherine McManamon, and Sam Herbert, "Information without Frontiers: Barriers and Solutions," *Insights* 28, no. 1 (2015): 64–68.

13. Peter Hernon and Ellen Altman, *Assessing Service Quality*, 2nd ed. (Chicago: American Library Association, 2010), 54.

14. Ibid., 55.

15. Marianne Stowell Bracke et al., "Finding Information in a New Landscape: Developing New Service and Staffing Models for Mediated Information Services," *College and Research Libraries* 68, no. 3 (2007): 253–54.

16. Ibid., 254.

17. Ibid., 255.

18. Susan Beatty and Claudette Cloutier, "More Questions than Answers: Using an Observational Study to Count Reference Activity," in *Leading the Reference Renaissance: Today's Ideas for Tomorrow's Cutting Edge Services*, ed. Marie L. Radford (New York: Neal-Schuman, 2012), 135.

Chapter Eight

Accepting How Reference Resources Necessarily Shape Reference Services

As reference collections move away from print and toward electronic resources, the ways reference services can be offered are also changing, opening the door to many ways to engage the patron. Although print reference collections have not entirely disappeared, the remaining print collections are much smaller than they formerly were. Electronic reference collections are growing as the print collections diminish. Since reference is no longer tied to print, the librarian can be anywhere and still assist a patron. Yet the reference librarian is still needed even when the resources are all electronic. Reference resources often require some knowledge and skill to use effectively. A patron on their own will often find it difficult to use an electronic resource or might not even find the electronic resource that will be the most useful.

This chapter covers planning and budgeting of reference resources, selecting and acquiring reference resources as well as the types of resources available, using a reference collection, weeding the reference collection, assessing the reference collection, and promoting it. It also discusses the advantages and disadvantages of electronic reference collections and how libraries can get the most for their money. The chapter concludes with a look at how the electronic reference collections are changing reference.

PLANNING AND BUDGETING

Planning and budgeting for an electronic resource collection differs from print resources. Print purchases have an upfront cost, but that is essentially the only cost for the life of the volume. Electronic resources are more complicated as the nature of library collections have shifted from ownership to access. An electronic resource that includes encyclopedias, dictionaries, handbooks, manuals, and so forth has both an upfront cost and an annual subscription fee for maintaining it. Many electronic resources are updated continuously or at least annually, but some are not. Even those with little updating charge a maintenance fee. These fees are not inexpensive. In addition to the electronic reference resources, libraries must also buy electronic journal titles and databases. Depending on the subject area, prices can be moderate or exorbitantly expensive. As a result, libraries are experiencing what has been deemed a "serials" crisis, in which journal subscription costs have outpaced inflation and databases, especially in STEM, are also extremely expensive. In turn, libraries experience a decrease in purchasing power, represented by the amount of resources and the amount of money libraries have to purchase or subscribe to them. For this reason, libraries must often cancel certain subscriptions to accommodate for these price increases.

Budgeting has to allow for annual increases in electronic resource costs. So the library has to be prepared to handle increasing costs or be prepared to cancel subscriptions that become too costly. Many libraries join consortia that handle electronic resource subscriptions. These consortia can reduce the subscription prices by having one subscription for a group of libraries, thus keeping the increases at a more reasonable level. Other benefits of consortia membership include smaller libraries having access to additional resources. A drawback to consortia membership is that a library may be subject to the demands of all other consortia members, which may result in the library paying for resources they do not need. Vendors have more than one way to charge for electronic resource subscriptions including FTEs (a fixed price based on the number of full-time equivalent students), simultaneous use (the number of individuals who can use the resource at the same time), and a flat fee. One way to determine which agreement works best for the library is through evaluation and assessment, specifically of usage statistics. Through these statistics, libraries can determine how many patrons are using each resource and what is the best subscription plan.

Handling electronic resources calls for a great deal of planning as well as working closely with vendors and other libraries. Increasing costs are inevitable so that libraries have to make difficult decisions on an annual basis just to stay even. Sometimes there is some negotiation room with the vendor or a better price if the library can renew for multiple years if they are allowed to do this. Planning is paramount.

According to Daniel Liestman, reference needs its own collection-development policy to articulate a plan to maintain balance in the collection in regard to format and content and to manage the size and growth of the collection.[1] Creating a collection-development policy for reference resources is an important consideration. It can describe both the formats the library will collect and the content it considers most important.

Reference resources differ from other parts of the collection due to their unique role in the library and their increased costs. They provide resources that are consulted but usually not read in their entirety and form the backbone of a collection that includes encyclopedias, dictionaries, handbooks, bibliographies, and databases. Many of these cost several times more than a single book.

Even if a formal collection-development policy for the library has not been developed, it is still important for libraries to have a reference collection-development plan. Without a plan, there is no way for libraries to coordinate the development of the reference collection. Many issues come up as purchases are made, such as the level of collecting in the library, subject areas and formats that have priority, and whether a particular title will be purchased in print or online. These decisions need to be documented so there will be consistency in the development of the reference collection. If not, this can lead to confusion as to the goals of the collection.

Some issues that should be addressed in a reference collection-development policy or plan include the following:

1. The selection of reference resources. It might describe how the selection of reference resources will be made. For example, some purchases may be made by a librarian in charge of that area. Then there might be a librarian committee who is in charge of making the final decisions for resources beyond a certain price. If the library belongs to a consortium, it must be clear how the library will interact with the consortium.

2. The acquisition of materials—both purchases and subscriptions. This issue can include how decisions about which resources to buy or subscribe to will be made. It might describe the kinds of formats and the content of the resources the library will acquire. It could also list the kinds of e-resources and databases that might be subscribed to as well as whether audio and video reference resources and data sets will also be acquired. Perhaps the library will want to make a statement about how it will select and handle open-access resources.

3. The size of the reference collection. Does the library expect the electronic reference collection to grow, or do they expect it to remain fairly stable allowing for titles to be added and deleted? This affects future planning and budgeting as well as selection.

4. Duplication. Will the library always opt to acquire a resource in its electronic format when available, or does the library foresee instances when they might want another format as well or choose the print version?

5. Assessment of the collection. The plan should discuss the periodic assessment of the collection and both how it will be done and the

criteria for it. Will it be an internal assessment using use statistics, or might it include a patron survey or focus group? What will be the goal of the assessment?

6. Weeding or deselection of the print collection and electronic materials. This document can describe how weeding or deselection will be done. Criteria for weeding or deselection need to be articulated. A statement about off-site storage could also be useful for print materials.

7. Cooperation. It is important to recognize groups that the library works with on collection development that might share electronic resources or have other cooperative acquisition arrangements.

ACQUISITION AND SELECTION OF RESOURCES

The process of selection is different when many materials are electronic. To be sure, some reference sources are still available in print, but many are only available electronically and may never have been available as print reference resources. One factor that hampers the selection of electronic reference resources is the limited number of reviews from sources such as *Library Journal*, *Choice*, and *Booklist*. Although reference books have never received widespread reviews, even less electronic resources are reviewed. Such a lack of reviews constitutes a problem given that many electronic resources are quite expensive and need careful consideration. Due to this expense, it is important for librarians to know the content of a resource and how it compares to similar resources. While it might not make a huge difference in a library's budget to have several print reference books with similar content that are reasonably priced, selection becomes more important when the resource price is higher and the library must pay an annual maintenance fee for electronic resources.

Another complication concerning selection is that it can be hard for the librarian to know of all the choices of available electronic resources and how to preview them. Although many publishers allow for a preview period of electronic resources, librarians may not have time to review all the options, given that this review can be more time consuming than reviewing print resources. Reviewing a print resource can often be accomplished quickly by scanning sections of the book. But electronic resources are simply slower as the librarian reviews different parts of the resource. If the librarian does not review electronic resources carefully before licensing them and ends up with a title with similar content, the library will have spent money needlessly. Therefore, the librarian's selection of electronic resources must be more careful and thus more time consuming. Many libraries use staff committees to select more expensive electronic resources to ensure a thoughtful decision with several points of view. Libraries also try to prevent duplication of resources because it has become apparent that such duplication is not cost effective and confuses patrons. To counter the multitudinous, often overwhelming in quantity, and uncurated offerings of commercial search engines, such as Google, the library should offer a lean, well-selected electronic reference collection. Yet for the sake of patron convenience engendered by these search engines, libraries should offer the ability to search multiple resources at the same time using a federated searching software or a discovery tool.

Although electronic resources are sometimes very expensive, especially electronic databases, reference resources also include open-access materials and primary source collections. This inclusion must further change the librarians' approach to selection. Specifically, open-access resources must be evaluated to determine if they should be listed as an additional resource or substitute for more expensive ones. It appears that libraries continue to struggle with these decisions. Based on the lack of extant research and case studies concerning selection of open-access materials, it will take more time to develop good guidelines regarding this selection. What existing findings on open-access materials, in general, indicate is that the quality of the resources is variable. Two good strategies libraries can employ in evaluating these resources or in providing reference instruction to others about them is to refer to Beall's list, which annually updates predatory open-access journals, as well as to caution patrons that Google Scholar indexes open-access journals that are of varying quality. Another suggestion is for academic libraries to build institutional repositories that provide open access to materials published by students and faculty. As libraries and archives digitize and collect primary documents and make them available to the public, another challenge posed is a marketing one. How are libraries to let their patrons know about these valuable collections? This question is addressed later in this chapter.

Many resources digitized from print are similar in content to their print counterparts, but the structure of the resource changes from print to electronic. Some of the information conveyed within print resources can be lost. Unless the library provides a description of the resource, there is little way to convey information, such as subjects covered and dates of coverage, to patrons. This lack of information for electronic resources makes it imperative that the librarians understand the content of each electronic resource and describe it to their patrons. To be sure, search interfaces for electronic resources provide ways of searching not captured by search tools for physical resources. For instance, a patron can search within the full text of a digital resource. However, if patrons are searching a database not appropriate to their subject of interest or searching another digital resource that is not a database, the search may produce only frustration.

Although print reference collections are getting smaller, there are a number of reasons print reference collections continue to exist. Patrons often expect to find a print reference collection when they visit the library and in fact prefer to use the print. Sometimes it is faster and easier to use a print reference book to browse more quickly and to find ideas serendipitously. Librarians often still choose print because the print version of a reference book is less expensive and is in a subject area that does not change very much. An example of this is a multivolume encyclopedia of biographies of people who are deceased.[2] Many libraries simply do not have the budget to buy every reference source they want as an electronic resource. Also some reference sources are not enhanced by being electronic so for those using the library they are just as good in print as in the electronic version.

The following are guidelines for selecting electronic resources:

1. Select a mix of multidisciplinary resources and resources specific to subject areas often requested by the patrons.
2. Try for a minimum of overlap. Too many similar electronic resources on the same subject can be confusing to the patron.
3. Use a federated search software or a discovery tool to make it easier for patrons to find information. Patrons like one-stop searching.
4. Compare similar resources carefully to get the most for the money. Find out the track record for various electronic resources such as how

Figure 8.1. Books and electronic resources are both part of reference collections.

much they usually raise their prices annually and how often they update the resource. Consider open-access resources.

5. Consider joining a consortium that does electronic resource licensing for a group of libraries to get better pricing so that the library can offer a larger number of electronic resources.

6. Think about how to market a particular electronic resource in advance of the subscription.

DISCOVERY TOOLS

Web-scale discovery tools provide a means to help patrons locate appropriate electronic resources. They provide a single way to search the collection using a central index. This index contains metadata records that have been extracted, or preharvested, from various collections to which the library has access. These discovery tools can be used to search across these collections, which may be localized, open access, and subscription based, using an interface that resembles that of a commercial search engine.[3] Increasingly, these tools have started to offer additional services beyond searching, such as curation. For instance, for some search queries one of the first results will be a research guide pertaining to the query rather than a relevant resource. Examples of web-scale discovery tools include EDS (EBSCO Discovery Service), Serials Solutions' Summon (ProQuest), and Primo Central Index (Ex Libris).

Discovery tools are solving some of libraries' problems for patrons who want one box to put in their terms and do their search. They can search books, articles, newspapers, and so forth, all at the same time. This ability carries the advantage of breaking down some of the academic silos that can be created when patrons search subject databases and may be a good tool for interdisciplinary researchers. However, research-evaluating discovery tools indicate issues with their usability. Although the tools look like a search engine, they do not search or present results in the same way. For this reason, patrons of discovery tools can experience confusion when their search results do not match their search terms in ways they anticipated. In addition, patrons expect that they will only need to look at the first page of search results to gather relevant sources, much like a search engine. Another issue with these search tools is that they tend to prefer displaying their own content. This preference may not be intentional but rather a result of the search tool being designed and trained on content owned by the company creating it. For these reasons, it is important that the discovery tools are well structured to provide guidance to the patron. For example, if a discovery tool searches many newspapers, it may be hard for patrons to identify the more substantive peer-reviewed articles. Discovery tools generally grant libraries varying capabilities to personalize their interfaces, which allows provision of information that signifies such guidance to patrons. In addition, reference instruction must be provided to address some of the usability issues with using these tools. Namely, Andrew Asher, Lynda Duke, and Suzanne Wilson studied how eighty-seven undergraduates used Summon and the EBSCO Discovery Service, among other search tools, and found that regardless of the tool, students depended on its default search settings. For this reason, reference instruction should detail how search settings affect what types of results are retrieved and how these results might differ based on the specific search tool used.[4]

USING ELECTRONIC RESOURCES

Electronic reference collections such as encyclopedias, dictionaries, subject encyclopedias, and databases have shaped how librarians assist patrons. In some ways the patrons need more help since the names of the resources and databases do not always adequately describe the contents, which may include audio and video as well as text. In these cases, it is up to the librarian to identify the databases and resources that a patron will find most helpful. Despite having access to multiple collections when using discovery tools or federated searching software, the patron may still need some help getting started and may need help going beyond the discovery tools, especially more deeply into one academic area.

On the positive side, services run in conjunction with access to electronic services, such as virtual reference services, allow the librarian to assist patrons regardless of where the individual is located. For example, the patron can start by texting the library to get information. The information may be quite easy to supply with a return text or the librarian may want to move the dialog to another medium, such as chat or telephone, to answer the question properly. Perhaps it is simply not possible to answer the question fully in text.

ASSESSMENT OF REFERENCE COLLECTIONS

Print reference collections are assessed both by subject knowledgeable librarians and by experienced reference librarians. Both use and currency are important factors in deciding if a particular resource should stay in the reference collection or be moved into the circulating collection. The use of electronic resources can be assessed by the statistics usually provided by the vendor. Issues beyond use are more difficult to assess. For instance, over time the appropriateness of an electronic resource in the library's reference collection may wane. Libraries may discover that some electronic resources get very little use and that most questions can be answered through another electronic resource. Also, as more electronic resources become available, the library may want to drop one title and acquire another based on a variety of factors, including subjects covered, number of periodical titles indexed, depth of indexing, and ease of use. Cost may also play a role in whether all electronic acquisitions can be maintained. There are many similar electronic resources available now so the library can choose one that both fits the patrons' needs and is fairly priced.

WEEDING REFERENCE COLLECTIONS

Weeding continues to play a role in the development of reference resource collections. Weeding should have basic criteria and be used consistently. These criteria apply to both print and electronic resources. We are used to weeding print resources that are out of date, in poor condition, no longer of interest to the patrons, or with inaccurate content. Electronic resources must also be weeded. The criteria are slightly different from print materials. If a resource is not updated regularly, it may not be providing the most recent information. Patrons think that an electronic resource must be up to date, so when it is slow in updating, it may not be of use. The interest in a particular

Figure 8.2.   Databases are an important part of electronic resources.

subject may have changed so that the resource is no longer being used or a new resource on the subject is available that is more appealing to the patrons because it is easier to use and more up to date. Sometimes the library subscribes to a resource because it is the only one on a subject, but as time goes on better resources on the same subject are available. So electronic resources can be weeded too as priorities and costs change.

PROMOTION OF REFERENCE COLLECTIONS

Developing a plan for promoting the reference collection is of prime importance. Reference is undoubtedly the most expensive part of the library's collection, so the library will want to encourage its use. Electronic collections can be completely invisible to patrons so it is up to librarians to bring them to the attention of the patrons. To promote the collection, the librarian should be sure that electronic resources are listed in the catalog and that it is as easy as possible for patrons to access the electronic resources. Many libraries choose to promote their databases and other electronic resources on their web pages. Others provide lists of electronic resources by subject with descriptions of each resource. Demonstrations of electronic resources at meetings and classes can help to promote underutilized resources. Featuring new resources on the library's web page is another good way to encourage use.

Laura Wallis describes the way the library at the University of Montevallo (Alabama) decided to promote its electronic resources. It developed a Virtual Reference Shelf (VRS) with LibGuides. The VRS has both a list of electronic resources title by title and then subject by subject. This was particularly useful when doing information-literacy classes since the librarian could point to a particular LibGuide or even develop a special LibGuide for the class.[5]

HOW ELECTRONIC COLLECTIONS ARE CHANGING REFERENCE

Electronic collections have changed the face of reference service since they can be accessed from almost anywhere. Once patrons know of their existence they can use them any time and any place. But it has also changed the work of the librarian. Many patrons need help both identifying appropriate electronic resources to use and using the resource. Librarians need to be vocal about their desire to assist patrons in identifying and using electronic resources. Demonstrations of different resources can give the patrons an idea of the kinds of information available and how to find what they are looking for. Librarians should never assume that using electronic resources is easy. A great deal of practice is involved in getting comfortable with electronic resources. When patrons see a long list of electronic resources, they are no doubt very confused as to how to decide which one to use. Many have trouble understanding bibliographical citations and cannot distinguish between books, periodical articles, newspaper articles, and other resources. A great deal of knowledge is needed, which is the reason reference librarians are so important in assisting the patron.

Table 8.1.

Feature	Definition	Tools
Access		
Single point of entry	Has the capability to search across all library resources. (Note: Although they have the ability, the five listed search tools do not provide 100% coverage due to varying vendor agreements.)	EBSCO Discovery Service, Encore, Primo, Summon, and WorldCat Local
Persistent links	Provides a stable, permanent link to a resource	AquaBrowser, Axiell Arena, Blacklight, EBSCO Discovery Service, and WorldCat Local
Mobile compatibility	At the very least, the service can be viewed and used on a mobile phone.	AquaBrowser, Axiell Arena, BiblioCommons, Blacklight, EBSCO Discovery Service, Encore, Endeca, Enterprise, eXtensible Catalog, Primo, Summon, Visualizer, VuFind, and WorldCat Local Blacklight, Enterprise, and eXtensible Catalog do not have a separate mobile interface but are accessible on mobile phones.
Functional requirements for bibliographic retrieval (FRBR)	Provides a link to different formats, editions, etc., of a work	eXtensible Catalog, Primo, and WorldCat Local
Aesthetic		
State-of-the-art interface	Presents with a simple search box and interface similar to commercial sites, e.g., Google, Amazon	AquaBrowser, Axiell Arena, BiblioCommons, Blacklight, EBSCO Discovery Service, Encore, Endeca, Enterprise, eXtensible Catalog, Primo, Summon, Visualizer, VuFind, and WorldCat Local
Search		
Simple keyword search	With advanced search option. Should be on each page. (Note: Due to the confusion a single search box can	AquaBrowser, Axiell Arena, BiblioCommons, Blacklight, EBSCO Discovery Service, Encore, Endeca,

Feature	Description	Products
	bring about, particularly if users do not recognize that advanced search capabilities are available to them, most libraries do not enable this feature.)	Enterprise, eXtensible Catalog, Primo, Summon, Visualizer, VuFind, and WorldCat Local eXtensible Catalog and Enterprise do not have the search box on each page.
Faceted navigation	Can narrow search results based on categories	AquaBrowser, Axiell Arena, BiblioCommons, Blacklight, EBSCO Discovery Service, Encore, Endeca, Enterprise, eXtensible Catalog, Primo, Summon, Visualizer, VuFind, and WorldCat Local
Spell checking	Offers search term suggestions for popularly misspelled terms	AquaBrowser, Axiell Arena, BiblioCommons, EBSCO Discovery Service, Encore, Endeca, Enterprise, Primo, Summon, Visualizer, VuFind, and WorldCat Local
Autocompletion/stemming	Completes search terms automatically as they are being typed based on popularly used search terms	Axiell Arena, Endeca, Enterprise, eXtensible Catalog, Summon, and WorldCat Local
Relevancy	Ranking algorithm considers factors other than topic relevance, including circulations and multiple copies.	Primo
Enriched content	Includes additional information within a document record including reviews, user-generated tags, cover images, etc.	AquaBrowser, Axiell Arena, BiblioCommons, Blacklight, EBSCO Discovery Service, Encore, Endeca, Enterprise, eXtensible Catalog, Primo, Summon, Visualizer, VuFind, and WorldCat Local BiblioCommons and AquaBrowser have the most features, and Blacklight, EBSCO Discovery Service, Endeca, and eXtensible Catalog have the least features.
User contribution	Includes some form of user input, e.g., reviews and rating	BiblioCommons offers input of the most user-supplied data.

		AquaBrowser, Axiell Arena, Encore, Primo, VuFind, and WorldCat Local offer some input for user-supplied data.
RSS feeds	Provides an RSS feed to allow patrons to monitor when records are added	AquaBrowser, Axiell Arena, EBSCO Discovery Service, Endeca, Enterprise, Primo, Summon, and VuFind
Integration with social media	Allows users to share library records with friends on social media sites	AquaBrowser, Axiell Arena, BiblioCommons, EBSCO Discovery Service, Encore, Endeca, eXtensible Catalog, Primo, and WorldCat Local
Recommendations	Makes recommendations to users based on information they have inputted, e.g., search terms; information from the library, e.g., circulation statistics; and other users, e.g., other documents checked out by users who checked out displayed document	Axiell Arena, BiblioCommons, EBSCO Discovery Service, Encore, Endeca, eXtensible Catalog, Summon, VuFind, and WorldCat Local make recommendations based on bibliographic data. Primo makes recommendations based on usage data.

Source: The fifteen features are derived from Breeding 2007; Murray 2008; Yang and Wagner 2010; and Chickering and Yang 2014. The definitions are derived from Yang and Wagner 2010; and Chickering and Yang 2014. The tools are derived from Chickering and Yang 2014.

NOTES

1. Daniel Liestman, "Reference Collection Management Policies: Lessons from Kansas," *College and Undergraduate Libraries* 8, no. 1 (2001): 85–121.

2. Naomi Lederer, "Why Libraries Should Retain a Core Print Reference Collection," *Reference Librarian* 57, no. 4 (2016): 307–22.

3. Michael Courtney, "Discovery Tools," in *Reimagining Reference in the 21st Century*, ed. David A. Tyckoson and John G. Dove (West Lafayette, IN: Purdue University Press, 2015), 123.

4. Andrew D. Asher, Lynda M. Duke, and Suzanne Wilson, "Paths of Discovery: Comparing the Search Effectiveness of EBSCO Discovery Service, Summon, Google Scholar, and Conventional Library Resources," *College and Research Libraries* 74, no. 5 (2012): 464–88.

5. Laura Wallis, "Building a Virtual Reference Shelf," *Serials Librarian* 67, no. 1 (2014): 52–60.

Chapter Nine

Preparing to Better Serve Our Patrons Today and Tomorrow

Chapter by chapter, this book discusses the many ways that reference work is changing. Although the physical desk has not completely disappeared, librarians are reaching their patrons in a variety of ways beyond it—within the library using a tiered reference model, roving reference, and a variety of technology and social media, as well as beyond the walls of the library, where librarians answer patron questions regardless of location, providing both face-to-face services and those mediated using Twitter, texting, instant messaging, and other social media. Such changes to reference services are a product of shifting patron expectations in a world of changing formats and means of communication. Many patrons search Google for information and may not patronize the library for traditional reference assistance. Such patrons expect information to be delivered to them expediently and are willing to sacrifice content quality for convenience in attaining information that is "good enough." Yet there is still a need for library services. Among Americans under age thirty surveyed by a 2014 Pew study, 62 percent agreed there is "a lot of useful, important information that is not available on the internet."[1]

All this change means that patrons expect more from the library than information provision if they are going to continue to use it. Traditional ways of doing business are not enough. To engage patrons with reference services, librarians must provide services above and beyond what a search engine can do. These include providing personalized service and assistance in doing more advanced research, assistance in identifying needed resources no matter where they are, and other value-added services. What these services have in common is that they address a shifting reference model that provides patrons with assistance at their point of need. By embracing this shift at a time when many services are becoming automated, libraries can continue to provide services relevant to each patron's need.

One way librarians can embrace shifting reference models is to examine reference as comprised of six perspectives outlined by VanScoy: information provision, instruction, communication, relationship building, guidance/advising, counseling, and partnerships.[2] These perspectives make it clear that information provision is just one of the areas of work for reference librarians.

INFORMATION PROVISION

Information provision is at the heart of what librarians do and what is expected of them. Librarians are experts at information provision, whether it is answering a ready reference question, helping with a term paper, or finding resources for a doctoral dissertation. Google has not supplanted this role. Rather, the disintermediation search engines introduced only stresses the importance of having trained professionals who can navigate vast information landscapes. It also cannot be assumed that all patrons will turn to Google for this service.

Librarians can often offer this service in a way that produces more indepth results than a search-engine results page due to their expertise in forming search strategies and evaluating information. But information provision is not limited to content delivery. Rather, there is an instructional component to this provision. When providing information to patrons, librarians show the patrons how they found the content. However, librarians should help them even beyond just showing them how to use a database. Librarians might help patrons develop a search strategy, and once the results are in, they can point out reliable journals and authors of interest. This assistance is not the same as helping patrons complete their entire research projects. But patrons are often overwhelmed at a list of bibliographic citations and can use some help deciding where to begin. Thus the importance of the librarian's role as mediator is more crucial than ever and inextricably linked to information provision.

INSTRUCTION

Instruction was introduced to the library world after information provision. Initially, instruction was comprised of one-to-one teaching as the librarian made transparent the process of finding the information requested by patrons. This process has become further complicated as the ways information can be searched have increased (see chapter 5). To address patron expectations for "one-stop shopping" for information, discovery tools represent the latest trend adopted by libraries to offer a search experience that parallels Google. With the introduction of tools that comb through mass amounts of information, librarians have had to change their information instruction methods. Librarians must emphasize the tools' relative merits and disadvantages. These may be hard to describe, however, since the content that is provided by these search tools and how it is presented may be opaque to the librarians as well as the patrons. For this reason, it is beneficial for librarians to inform patrons that this opacity exists and to emphasize how the default search settings, which patrons are most likely to use, will affect how their results are presented and how this presentation will vary by search tool. [3]

Aside from providing individual instruction, librarians found it was efficient to teach groups of patrons about the library. The group could be a class at the college or university level or an elementary school class visiting the public library to learn more about the resources available to them. Instruction has grown tremendously and with it more of a need to perfect the librarian's skills in this area. Librarians have learned how to craft their instruction style to fit the situation. Since not all classes are the same, the message must change depending on the group. Librarians have learned more about presentation skills and how to engage groups to get their message across, when discussing how to use the best resources and the library effectively. Classes also help to market library resources and library services by making the patrons more comfortable with the librarian and willing to visit the library for follow-up.

COMMUNICATION AND RELATIONSHIP BUILDING

Since many patrons anticipate information provision without mediation from a librarian, librarians who provide reference services to these patrons have the opportunity to articulate the value of the librarian as mediator. One of the ways this value can be articulated is by developing rapport to open lines of communication with the patron. It is essential that librarians make sure patrons feel welcomed, and their information needs are considered very important. Relationship building follows communication. It describes how librarians work with patrons and, over time, develop their trust. Patrons need to feel that the librarian is focused on their problem and ready to help. If librarians only provide basic services, then patrons may feel they do not need the librarian. But if librarians take a real interest in patrons, then patrons will want to return for further assistance. One of the ways librarians can take such an interest is by following up with patrons following the initial reference interview to see if patrons need additional help or have a new information need. Relationship building to instill patrons with confidence in librarians is an important part of the process.

GUIDANCE AND COUNSELING

When using search engines patrons are used to an information environment where resources are innumerable and the way in which they are organized is opaque. It can be a relief to patrons to interact with collections that contain a discrete number of carefully curated items that follow a more transparent organizational schema. One of the ways librarians build relationships with their patrons is by guiding them in using these collections. It is librarians, who know the collections and how information within them is organized, who can guide patrons in finding the very best resources. Once patrons become familiar with navigating certain collections, they may find it is easier for them to navigate information within the collection than by using a search engine. For this reason, librarians must always be ready to find the time to help patrons make their way through the many available resources.

Counseling follows guidance and denotes the librarian helping the patron in a more hands-on way. Counseling services now offered in many libraries include personalized research consultations. In these consultations the librarian works one to one with patrons, helping the patrons to define their problem and then assisting them to find appropriate materials to resolve their problem. These services have enhanced the way librarians work with patrons, as librarians go beyond just identifying resources that might be useful to actually helping the patron find them and evaluate them.

COLLABORATIONS AND PARTNERSHIPS

Partnerships are an important word in an expanding library vocabulary. Partnerships can be between librarians and patrons, librarians and other librarians, and librarians and other institutions. Librarians working in partnership with patrons develop a balance of power and expertise. When librarians allow patrons to have a say in what and how information is delivered to them, there is a more equitable exchange that ultimately provides patrons with information relevant to their needs.[4]

Librarians can work with each other in several ways. As discussed in chapter 2, new models of reference, such as triage, involve communication between librarians to ensure that the appropriate level of service is being performed based on the patron's point of need. Collaboration is also afforded by social media channels, such as librarians using Twitter to address reference queries that may be outside their scope of expertise, or the increasing globalization of virtual reference services.

Working with institutional or community groups makes the library more visible and relevant to its community. This communication is especially important given that individuals often perceive the library as symbolically valuable but are unaware of the specific services it provides. By partnering with groups that afford access to the community the library serves, libraries have an important channel to raise awareness of their functions and services.

CREATIVITY AND INNOVATION

Based on the discussions throughout the book, it can be concluded that libraries and librarians must go beyond the basics of reference services, that is, information provision. So what concrete steps can librarians take to accomplish this task? Steven Bell has written about the patrons' experience when they visit the library, stating that the patrons should expect more than just a transaction. Specifically, the patron experience should be different, memorable, and evoke loyalty. It should differentiate the library from a search engine. To this end, Bell identified some reference strategies to make the patron experience a better one. These strategies include the following:

1. Start with core values. The core values of reference are to understand the patrons' questions and then assist them in finding the information they need.
2. Personalize to create meaning. Personalize the service to provide assistance that the patron needs and expects.
3. Meet the patrons' needs. Sometimes meeting patrons' needs means going beyond what they articulate. Consider a patron who needs information for a book he or she is writing and, following the reference interview, explains that the book will be self-published. The librarian can then provide information on what is involved in self-publishing a book, including finding a publisher, a freelance editor, and a marketing consultant.
4. Anticipate the patrons' needs. As in the example above, patrons may not have initially articulated all of their needs, so the librarian should be thinking ahead as to what the patrons might need.
5. Motivate and empower staff. It is vital that the staff members feel they are supported in using their own good judgment beyond the basics of information provision.
6. Create emotional connections. Personalization of services will often help to create emotional connections to patrons, which will encourage their repeat visits to the library. If the patrons leave with more than they expected, they will want to return more often.
7. Aim for totality. This stage can be thought of as the librarian packaging information so that the patrons have as much or as little as they need.[5]

Looking more closely at each of these strategies, the first one, core values, is one practiced by librarians every day. But this stage cannot solely be addressed at the beginning of the reference interview. If it is, then the librarian only offers provision of information as a service. As discussed above, there are other services that the librarian must provide, and further, provision of information has shifted to address the patron's point of need. Certainly at the beginning, librarians should take time to understand the patron's initial question and assist him or her in finding necessary resources. This skill is what librarians have been taught to do when performing reference services, and they do it well. But capturing the totality of a patron's information need may not happen in one encounter. Patrons may not have fully thought through their problem and, only after looking at some resources, do they get a better idea of what help they need. For this reason, librarians need to figure out how to meet patron needs not only as they begin their work but also as they continue pursuing their information need or needs. Follow-up may include several visits by the patron to the librarian. It is important for the patron to understand that follow-up visits are expected, rather than a burden on the librarian.

The second strategy concerns personalizing the reference experience. Patrons should feel they are special and the help the librarian provides is tailored to their needs, rather than the provision of a routine answer. Patrons often positively regard personalization as a service provided by search engines and other social media tools. However, many recognize that this personalization also comes with significant caveats related to privacy. Librarians can add distinct value to their services by providing personalization without these caveats. Personalization of reference services constitutes an important part of the librarian's job, which can help to solidify the patron's relationship with the library. The librarian can help the patron to find the exact kind of materials that will be useful for the patron's project.

The third strategy is meeting the patron's needs. This can be in one session or in a series of consultations, particularly if the patron has a research project. Although some patron needs can be dealt with in one session, the librarian should welcome follow-up contact. Further, the librarian should always be thinking about possible value-added services that may be welcomed by the patron. Unlike search engines, where the scope of the collection remains unknown, librarians are aware of the vast amount of information available in their institution's collection or collections, and it is their responsibility to share this knowledge with patrons.

The librarian should also engage in another strategy of anticipating patron needs. Librarians should be thinking ahead to identify resources that a patron will find of value. Such anticipation will be welcomed by the patrons and make them realize it is useful to stay in touch with the librarian. The librarian will want to indicate that they expect to have more requests for assistance from the patron and is planning for them. This future assistance might be a continuation of the information need or needs already presented by the patron or other ones.

Giving staff members the ability to use their own judgment when assisting patrons is very important. Some patrons need little assistance while others need much more. Having rules that hamper staff members' ability to do their best work by providing services personalized to specific patrons simply makes a bad impression on them. While guidelines for the staff are good, rigid rules are not. Staff members must feel free to locate other materials for the patron, wherever they are, and to make appropriate referrals. The staff should be allowed to go the extra mile when needed to get the patron needed resources.

A key strategy to retain patron visits to the library is by the librarian developing emotional connections with the patron. As indicated by studies overviewed in previous chapters, patrons often perceive the library as only being comprised of static information resources and are unaware of the additional services librarians can provide. When the patrons realize that the library is there to help them with their specific information need or needs, they will be encouraged to use the library's services. Further, by proactively establishing emotional connections with patrons, librarians can ensure future visits from them by circumventing the timidity of patrons who may be afraid to ask for more help or assistance.

Finally, Bell discussed how librarians should aim for totality. This statement implies that the librarian should provide as much information as the patron needs. If there are several facets to an inquiry, they should all be addressed. The librarian must make the patron feel that nothing is too much to ask and the librarian is always willing to provide more assistance. Further, totality represents more than the sum of the components described above. Rather, these components serve as a patron's entryway to an experience that must be carefully crafted by the library staff. Therefore, it is not enough for a librarian to address a single component and anticipate that they have provided value to their patrons. Rather, all of the components must be addressed, and the ways in which they are addressed must interact with one another to communicate a specific experience to the patron. Some of the ways these components can work together to communicate this specific experience will now be detailed.

In summarizing what these steps communicate, Bell contended that librarians need to do better in standing out, both within and outside of the library. One way to stand out, as Bell wrote with John Shank, is via "blended librarianship."[6] This approach envisions library work as "librarian centric" and "focused on [librarians'] skills, knowledge they have to offer and relationships they build."[7] The authors envisioned librarians in the academic world being the people who can coordinate between many players, such as instructional design people, technology people, and even faculty members, to help patrons make full use of the resources available. Librarians can identify the many resources available to students, the faculty, and the staff and provide access to them. These resources exceed the physical collection and include streaming video, podcasts, games, simulations, and Web 2.0 tools. [8]

Another voice discussing new ways of providing good library service is James LaRue, who provided a public library perspective. LaRue stated that librarians must be courteous, have content to deliver, and be visible to patrons. He also discussed the reference experience, which must be "more integrated and direct" in regard to how librarians approach patrons. [9] These facets of librarianship work to create a "transparent library that highlights both the presence and the value of the librarian. . . . [The] visible librarian is engaged, actively managing the relationship between the institution and patron to assure the highest quality results." [10] Transparency and visibility can be achieved by librarians providing more than just a list of resources that the patron then reads and evaluates. Rather, librarians should digest and summarize information, highlighting the important findings. This added value can manifest as an executive summary, for example. Librarians could also help patrons to create a profile of resources that they will find useful on an ongoing basis, preventing them from having to start the research process from scratch for each search session. To this end, many integrated library systems (ILS) allow for the development of an individual profile. [11]

ASSESSMENT AND EVALUATION

Where once librarians thought it was enough to have a good collection and provide resources to patrons, they now have a great deal of competition in these areas. Companies and services experiencing commercial success provide patrons with experience as well as the product. For libraries to determine what constitutes a positive patron experience, it is necessary to perform evaluation and assessment to discover what the patron expects and meet those expectations. Evaluation and assessment can be gauged using data-collection methods such as surveys, focus groups, and interviews (discussed in chapter 7).

Libraries must move beyond guessing what their patrons might like and collect information to determine what their patrons want. But performing data collection is hard because patrons often do not expect more from libraries than access to collections. To address these myopic expectations, librarians must find the right questions to ask that allow patrons to imagine a type of library different than one that is only collections based. Specifically, librarians must find out how patrons look for information and insert themselves into real-life, rather than idealized, situations of information seeking.

Libraries spend a great deal of money subscribing to databases that are often underutilized. Such underutilization by patrons may be due to the database interface not being easily usable for them. In light of the learning curve needed to navigate databases, how can the library make its services more accessible so that patrons will want to turn to the library rather than Google to get information? If people are willing to visit the library, how can the library make it such a pleasant experience that they will return? Does that mean helping people find what they need quickly so they can go on their way? Does it mean setting up an appointment where librarians create research profiles for patrons so they do not have to start at the beginning of the research process each time they come to the library or can continue to work on their areas of interest online? Does it mean that library hours are inconvenient and need to be changed? Does it mean that librarians should experiment with various technologies, such as Twitter, texting, and instant messaging, to see what will be useful to patrons? Libraries have often run for their own convenience and not the convenience of their patrons. All that needs to change now. In the field of information provision, businesses respond to what their patrons want and shape their goals and objectives accordingly. The world is fast paced, and time and convenience are extremely important.

Geraldine Torrisi-Steele and colleagues wrote about how librarians are even more needed in a world with an overwhelming amount of information. They stated that "librarians must understand the nature of research in a digital age" to better serve as guides and partners to their patrons.[12] They discussed the changing nature of research from the prevalence of sole authorship of journal articles to articles written by several people collaborating and from single subjects to multidisciplinary subjects. The authors also addressed the important role of the web and electronic resources, especially databases and e-journals. Of great interest is the emergence of new data sources, environments for conducting research, and ways of disseminating research such as via social media. Although the research methods may not be new, the same methods have moved from face-to-face to being repurposed and done virtually. Some of these repurposed methods include direct observation, surveys, focus groups, and interviews. New to research is the availability of a vast number of large data sets and the ability to do large-scale data analysis, text and data mining, iconographic tracking, and trend analysis. New tools are also available to access and process this data. The presence of these new capabilities calls on librarians to use their skills to help patrons work in this new environment.

MARKETING

Libraries and librarians must rebuild their image and way of doing business. This rebuilding means tuning in to the needs of current patrons and adjusting services to meet their needs. This adjustment may not be the same in every library or even by library type. It will be challenging to understand where a community of patrons lies in the continuum between self-service and the need for personalized service, and how libraries can best meet their needs. Meeting these needs can definitely be achieved by thinking outside of the box and not letting the four walls of the library define the mission of librarians.

Librarians must continually market their services. To do so they must engage more fully with their patrons, such as letting their patrons know what the library can make available to them, finding ways to shorten the research process for the patron in need of a quick solution, and making the library so visible that patrons will think of the library and its website before thinking of Google. Such engagement is a lot to ask but definitely needed. Having so many underused resources is simply not cost effective. We need to take a look at how the best companies are marketing their products and encouraging people to use their services. These approaches involve convenience, customer service, and a product people want.

CONCLUSION

In conclusion, library reference service must develop to satisfy the needs of today's patrons. Libraries must provide service that is convenient and saves the time of patrons as much as possible, making it easy for patrons to do their work. Impediments to all points of service need to be eliminated as much as possible, such as journals the patrons cannot access due to an embargo. Patrons want a user-friendly interface and immediate access to full-text articles. Databases and other resources that do not fulfill these requirements should be a thing of the past. Every resource must be easy to use and self-explanatory.

Librarians must be more than just experts in finding the correct answer in a reference book. They must instead be experts in understanding the information landscape and assisting patrons in finding the information they need in light of it. Librarians must be able to evaluate, analyze, and even summarize information as well as provide advice, guidance, and instruction to patrons. These abilities require a great deal of knowledge about information systems and how information is organized. Although these abilities may seem like a lot to ask from librarians, the future of reference services depends on librar-

Figure 9.1.   The future.

ians possessing them. Whether it is called reference service or by some other name, customer service has to be the focus of the future of libraries.

NOTES

1. Pew Research Center, "Younger Americans and Public Libraries," report, Washington, DC, 2014, http://www.pewinternet.org/.

2. Amy VanScoy, "Inventing the Future by Traditional and Emerging Roles for Reference Librarians," in *Leading the Reference Renaissance: Today's Ideas for Tomorrow's Cutting-Edge Services*, ed. Marie L. Radford (New York: Neal-Schuman, 2012).

3. Andrew D. Asher, Lynda M. Duke, and Suzanne Wilson, "Paths of Discovery: Comparing the Search Effectiveness of EBSCO Discovery Service, Summon, Google Scholar, and Conventional Library Resources," *College and Research Libraries* 74, no. 5 (2012): 464–88.

4. VanScoy, "Inventing the Future."

5. Steven J. Bell, "The Reference Patron Experience: It's Up to You to Design It," in *Leading the Reference Renaissance: Today's Ideas for Tomorrow's Cutting-Edge Services*, ed. Marie L. Radford (New York: Neal-Schuman, 2012), 19.

6. Steven J. Bell and John D. Shank, "Blended Librarianship: (Re)Envisioning the Role of Libraries in the Digital Information Age," *Reference and Patron Services Quarterly* 51, no. 2 (2011): 105–10.

7. Ibid.

8. Ibid.

9. James LaRue, "The Visibility and Invisibility of Librarians," *Library Journal* 135, no. 19 (2010): 10.

10. Ibid.

11. Ibid.

12. Geraldine Torrisi-Steele et al., "Research Goes Digital: Some Methods, Frameworks, and Issues," *Reference Librarian* 56, no. 4 (2015): 239–58.

Index

About the Author

Kay Ann Cassell is presently an assistant teaching professor at the School of Communication and Information, Department of Library and Information Science, at Rutgers University. Her areas of teaching and research include reference services and collection development. Cassell has been the director of several public libraries and an academic library as well as working as a reference librarian. She was associate director for collections and services of the branch libraries of the New York Public Library. She served in the Peace Corps in Morocco and was director of the Coordinating Council of Literary Magazines. She is active in the American Library Association and served as president of RUSA (Reference and User Services Association). Cassell has also been the editor of the quarterly journal *Collection Building*.